Woking Baptist Congregational

CHURCH

ON THE MOVE

Woking Baptist Congregational

CHURCH
ON THE MOVE

Published by John Gloster
Woking, Surrey, UK

Copyright © 2019 J Gloster

Second Edition, September 2019
Book production and cover design by Tony Lyttle
Printed by Kindle Direct Publishing

ISBN: 978-1-0772-0314-3

About the author

John Gloster is retired from his job as a research scientist with the Met Office. Married to Gill, they have three grown-up children and seven grandchildren. From childhood, he has attended the Church where his father, Leslie Gloster, was Church Treasurer for many years and a Church Elder. His great-grandfather, Henry William Gloster, was one of the original eight members who formed Woking Baptist Church in 1879.

To my wife, Gill, for her love and support over more than forty years and also to my three children, Chris, Katie and Vicky.

Woking Baptist Congregational

CHURCH

ON THE MOVE

1879 - 1999

A minute by minute account
of the first 120 years of

WELCOME CHURCH

written and compiled by

JOHN GLOSTER

All profits to Welcome Church, Woking

FORWARD
by Steve Petch

Life moves in seasons. Just when you think you've settled into a familiar routine, something changes: people enter or leave our lives; events surprise us; people make decisions that impact on us; we leave school, start work, move house, change jobs, get married, have children, make new friends, lose contact with others, experience sickness and bereavement and so much more.

Most seasons of my life so far have been kind; a few have been more challenging. There are many seasons of life I remember fondly; there are a few I would be quite happy to forget.

The same is true of our Church's life over the years, and as you read through this record of our history you will see that the Church has been through many different seasons. Many of these have been happy times; some have been more challenging.

There have been times of great blessing in our Church's history: powerful moves of the Holy Spirit, multiple baptisms, rapid growth, incredible giving, breakthroughs with buildings, lives being changed, Churches being planted, a deep sense of unity and mission together.

There have also been some challenging times: arguments and disagreements over trivial issues, accusations against leaders, crippling debt, two World Wars, leadership challenges and fall outs, people who have left, challenges with buildings, seasons with no apparent breakthrough in salvation and no one joining or being baptised. In 1897, the founding pastor, Edward Tarbox, 18 years after planting the Church and 6 years after moving on from it, had to come back for five months to save the Church from total collapse. There were some tough times!

All the way through the life of this Church, in good times and in bad, God has been consistently faithful. Jesus who said, *"I will build my church"* has been at work. He has never let go and has worked through the Church, despite many human failings, to bring salvation and new life to many, many people.

I have been the Lead Pastor at Welcome Church for just over two years now. I count it a privilege and I thank God for calling me here. When the time comes for me to finish and enter a new season, I hope to hand the role on well and cheer on whoever comes after me.

Right now we are in a season of rapid and exciting change that is affecting lots of areas of our life together as a Church. We are enjoying seeing our new building project move forward rapidly, and people have given sacrificially to see it done, yet the work is causing us huge disruption. Our nation is also in a time of rapid change and seems to be turning further from its Christian heritage every day; it's a challenge that we face on a daily basis. As a Church, now, as in the past, we are doing our best to discern the right way forward in all of this, and to follow the leading of Jesus. It's so encouraging to know that, even if we make some mistakes, Jesus won't let us slip or fall; he is at work in us and through us.

We recently finished preaching through the book of Philippians. I think we can say with certainty, just like the Apostle Paul did, that we are, *"confident of this, that he who began a good work in you will carry it on to completion until the day of Christ Jesus"* (Phil 1v6)

This has been seen to be true of our Church throughout its life, and therefore it's true of us individually as well, since the Church is made up of the individual people. Let's all lay hold of this truth for ourselves. You are not an exception; we are each known and loved by God. Even as we are reminded of our Church's past in the pages of this book, let us walk into the future together with confidence. Not a confidence based on our own abilities or resources, but a confidence based on the character of Jesus and his heart of love towards us as individuals and as a Church, and his heart of love towards the lost people of this town.

Steve Petch,

Lead Pastor, Welcome Church

September, 2019

ACKNOWLEDGEMENTS

I wish to thank Tony Lyttle, for his skilled help with the production of this book; Steve Petch and the leaders of Welcome Church for their encouragement to document the journey of the Church through the years and giving access to Church records; numerous Church members who, either in writing or verbally, have provided valuable insight into past events; Ordinance Survey for the use of the historic maps of Woking and to Richard and Rosemary Christophers for their help in producing Appendix A – Lest We Forget. Finally, I want to acknowledge the invaluable help of Gill Gloster, Anita Lyttle and Alice Potter who painstakingly proof-read the manuscript.

If anyone mentioned in the text would prefer their name to be omitted, it will be deleted in subsequent editions. And if any reader spots an error I would be more than willing to correct it in any subsequent revisions.

PREFACE

The material in this book was first produced as an A4 report in November 2009 entitled, *A Church on the Move – the history of The Coign Church 1879 to 1999*. It presented a chronological and detailed story of the Church over the years, as recorded in the Church minutes.

This new edition presents the same information in a more accessible format. Some additional material has also been included; for example, an appendix has been added giving details of those from our Church who died in the First or Second World Wars and another, about the development of music in worship through the years.

This book is a companion volume to *Welcome, Coign and Woking Baptist Church Story (December 2018)*, which provides an overview of more recent events as remembered by those involved. There is inevitably an overlapping period covered by both books and hence there is some duplication in a few places.

TABLE OF CONTENTS

TABLE OF CONTENTS

"We will not hide them from their descendants, we will tell the next generation the praiseworthy deeds of the Lord, his power, and the wonders he has done." (Psalm 78:4)

CHAPTER 1

INTRODUCTION

It is over 40 years since the TV drama "Roots" was first screened. The programme drew viewers' attention to the importance of understanding their own heritage. A more recent TV series traced celebrities' ancestors and this, together with other prompts, started me thinking about my own past and set me off on an enjoyable task of tracing my family roots. My own family has been involved with The Welcome Church, formerly called The Coign Church and before that, Woking Baptist Church since it was originally formed in 1879 as Woking Baptist Congregational Church. It was natural for me to start with Church records.

A further stimulus to explore local Church history came one evening at a Church House Group meeting. One of the members, Brian Bonnington, challenged me to document the history of the Church for the benefit of new Church members. The project began shortly afterwards.

With so many newcomers to the Church, only a few will have had the opportunity or even desire, let alone the access, to examine the records in order to try and decipher how God has been working His purposes out in the part of Surrey where we live. I have had that privilege and can conclude that we have a wonderful God who is skilfully building His Church ready for when He returns. He has never promised that He will make the way easy and this is clearly seen over the lifetime of the Church, which includes years of recession, wars, and a multitude of challenges both practical and spiritual. But despite these difficulties the Church has survived and indeed grown from less than ten members to currently over six hundred men, women and children in 2019.

In this account I have deliberately recorded events as they happened in a sequential format to highlight the importance of God's timing in building His Church. Major Church developments have deliberately been interspersed with some seemingly trivial issues and these reveal the workings of the Church at a much more practical level. The account cannot capture the full spiritual dimension of Church growth. This is often something personal to individuals and extremely difficult to re-create from formal accounts of Church meetings. Where memories are available, some detail has been included.

The period covered by this book has been limited to the years 1879 to 1999. More recent events are recorded in my companion volume, *Welcome, Coign and Woking Baptist Church Story (2018)*.

To avoid confusion when reading this document, it may be helpful to give some simple account of who is who in the Gloster family. Henry William Gloster was one of the founder members of the Woking Baptist Congregational Church. He had seven sons including Henry William (Junior), Dan, Charlie and Tom. Tom had a son called Leslie and my brother Colin and I are Leslie's sons. Put simply, the first Henry William is my great-grandfather.

CHAPTER 2

THE EARLY YEARS

Pastor: Edward William Tarbox 1879 to 1891

Prior to the 1830's, Woking as we know it today did **1830** not exist. In Edward Ryde's (1883) "History of Woking" it was described as "a purely agricultural parish of good average, quality and condition". Iain Wakeford (1987) describes the area around the current town centre as "a wasteland which stretched to the east as far as Byfleet, to the west as far as Hook Heath, St John's, Knaphill and Brookwood, to the south Heathside and the north Horsell. However, with the arrival of the train line in 1838 stretching from the south coast to London and passing through the area, the town started to develop very quickly".

1870 By the 1870's it is recorded that among much building work a Methodist chapel was built in 1872 and the Church of England had a corrugated iron building for worship (which was later replaced by Christ Church). See Appendix D, Figure 1 for a map of the area.

1879 During the summer of 1879 Edward William Tarbox, Pastor of Addlestone Baptist Church decided to explore the possibilities of establishing a Baptist Church presence in the rapidly growing town of Woking. He made enquires of some of the Christians who lived in the town and it was agreed to set up a Branch Mission Station under the care of Addlestone Baptist Church. It was decided to start by meeting in a villa in Goldsworth Road, and then look for freehold land on which to build a Church. Forty people attended the first meeting on Thursday 18 September 1879. This was followed on 28 September by the first Sunday service where Edward William Tarbox preached twice, the first Communion was held, and eight persons were welcomed into membership[1]; five transferred their membership from Penge (a suburb of London in the London Borough of Bromley) and three from Addlestone. It was decided that the Church would take on the name of "Woking Baptist Congregational Church". The following resolutions were passed on that first Sunday:

- Edward William Tarbox would become the first Pastor.
- The Church would be affiliated to Addlestone Baptist Church.
- Henry William Gloster (See Appendix D Figure 5) would become a Deacon and John Ashley the Sunday School Superintendent, initially for six months.

---

[1] Appendix C shows the numbers of baptisms and Church members through the years

- A committee would be convened to secure freehold ground for a building and then oversee the building of a small room for worship and general activities of the Church.

Oct 1879 On 3 October 1879 it was agreed to purchase a small piece of land in Goldsworth Road and build a small building, with room for expansion in the future (see Appendix D, Figure 6). The land was approximately one hundred and eighteen by forty feet, with the building occupying approximately forty by twenty-five feet. Two weeks later permission to go ahead with the building was obtained. The initial cost for the work was estimated to be around £300. Members of Addlestone Baptist Church agreed to contribute an initial £100 and new members from Woking £100. By

Feb 1880 10 February 1880 Rev Samuel and Edward William Tarbox laid the memorial stones in the partially erected building and on 15 March the building was formally opened for public services with an afternoon prayer and praise meeting, followed by a tea and public worship in the evening. The first sermon in the new building was preached by Rev William Brock, President of the London Baptist Association, his text being "The blood of Jesus Christ". The overall cost of the building work and furnishings came to £455; this left the Church with a debt of several hundred pounds which was not finally cleared until mid-1882.

The Church gradually began to grow with new members being added. Edward William Tarbox preached every Thursday evening and was available at the Church for anyone who wanted a "religious conversation". Thirty-eight chairs were purchased and rented out to members, thus raising a small source of revenue for the Church. In a similar way it was agreed to purchase and rent hymn books to members and have some spare for visitors. John Ashley agreed to lead singing and eventually began a psalmody class. By May 1881 weeknight meetings were moved to **May** Tuesdays, a prayer meeting held after Sunday evening **1881** services and evangelistic open airs held "when practical".

The Pastor was not only concerned about people who lived in Woking but was also interested in establishing a Church in the nearby village of Knap Hill (more recently spelt Knaphill). As such, his time was divided between Addlestone, Woking and Knap Hill. To help him with this large workload it was unanimously agreed by the members, totalling twenty-

1882 one at the end of 1882, to invite Mr A H Moore, of Ealing, to act as his assistant. He was invited to preach as frequently as was convenient but only paid expenses.

Until April 1882 Edward William Tarbox had given his services to the Church without payment. This changed following a Church meeting at which Henry William Gloster (Junior) proposed that from mid-summer the rent from seat hire and the weekly offering should be given to the pastor (seat and hymn book hire raised £7 10s 0d a quarter in 1882).

In the same summer, thoughts began to turn towards building a new chapel. However, there was still an outstanding debt of £7 12s 6d on the existing building. It was decided at a Church meeting to pass round an offering plate to clear the debt. This was done, and a new building fund opened with promises of £65 0s 0d.

In March 1883 Mrs Tarbox was received into **Mar** membership and this was taken as a sign that her **1883** husband's desire was to leave Addlestone and spend all his time in Woking; one month later this proved to be the case and he offered his services to the Church at Woking. This proposal was put to a Church meeting and it was unanimously agreed that he should be invited to become the dedicated Church pastor. One month later Henry William Gloster wrote to Addlestone Baptist Church withdrawing from direct union with them on the grounds that the Church was now able to become self-sufficient. This was favourably received, and they offered their harmonium, worth £40, for £10 (the cost of moving it). At the same time Edward William Tarbox was received into membership.

By October 1883 the Church at Woking, together with **Oct** that at Knap Hill totalled sixty-seven members (forty-**1883** three at Woking and twenty-four at Knap Hill).

Nov A major problem arose in November 1883 when **1883** Edward William Tarbox became dangerously ill. As a result, he offered his resignation, but this was not accepted by the members who hoped that he would recover. A temporary committee was set up to oversee the work under the leadership of Henry William Gloster. This continued in operation until the Pastor had recovered in April 1884. However, it was recognised that there were advantages in having a committee to help run the Church. Consequently, a consulting committee comprising the pastor, a deacon, superintendent, secretary and organist from Woking and the superintendent from Knap Hill was formed.

Jan In January 1884 Charlie Gloster presented the **1884** financial accounts; this was a change to the previous practice when they had been presented on Lady Day (Lady Day is the traditional name of the Feast of the

Annunciation of the Blessed Virgin - 25 March - The "Lady" was the Virgin Mary). One matter of significance was discussed at the meeting and that was that the tenders for the new Church vestry had been received. It was agreed to proceed, and the new room was opened on 30 March.

The main topic for discussion at the Church meeting **Apr** in April 1884 was the need to build a new chapel. **1884** Three members pledged £300 and a building committee was formed (Henry William Gloster treasurer, Henry William Gloster (Junior) and Charlie Gloster).

A less than helpful matter arose later during the spring. Questions were asked about the work at Knap Hill. The property where the meetings were held had been leased for three years by Edward William Tarbox from the Glosters and this agreement was due to expire during June 1884. Edward William Tarbox was **Jun** not sufficiently satisfied with the quarrelsome **1884** behaviour of the Knap Hill members. This had been drawn to their attention and a few had resigned. The deacon responsible for the Church offered to pay £20 for renovating the chapel and asked for the building to be free from rent for twelve months. Members at Woking decided unanimously that the work at Knap Hill should continue as a mission station, with members being counted as part of Woking Baptist Congregational Church. On 3 August twenty-nine people from Knap Hill joined the main Church in Woking, bringing the overall number to seventy. In July Edward William Tarbox discussed the possibility of F R Crewdson from Weybridge taking on some of the responsibility for the work at Knap Hill. He agreed to become the full-time assistant pastor, without charge. This was agreed by the Church and he became a member of the Woking Baptist Congregational Church and commenced his work on Sunday 23 August 1885.

Jun 1885 During June 1885 the Building Committee wrote to Peak's of Guildford and Chapman's of London asking them to draw up plans for the new chapel. Finance for the new building had started to be received, thanks to a weekly giving plan. However, members decided that further action was required, and it was agreed to have tickets for sale; these tickets representing bricks in the new building.

In September 1885 it was agreed that a "social **Sep** meeting" would be held later that month to discuss **1885** various recommendations of the Church Committee in respect to the Church and "aggressive work" during the coming winter. At this meeting, which commenced with prayer, a hymn and an address from the Pastor, it was unanimously decided to:

- Open branch preaching stations in selected localities.
- Establish a weekly prayer meeting prior to the start of the Sunday morning service.
- Form a Sunday afternoon Young Men's Bible Class.
- Organise a society with the object of providing readings, music and opportunities for debate

for the mutual improvement and entertainment of its members.

In the autumn of 1885 Edward William Tarbox's attention was drawn to the possibility of setting up a mission at The Bleak/ Anthony's (near the present Six Crossroads' Roundabout, Woodham). On investigation it was reported that "the folk were practically heathen, with the little-folk running wild, the people ignorant of the gospel and their elders mostly engaged in gardening and debauchery". The nearest place of worship or school was two miles away. It was agreed to hire a disused shop every **Dec** Sunday afternoon. The first service was held on 6 **1885** December when fourteen attended the main meeting and twenty-seven the Sunday School. Within six months problems with space were encountered as forty children were attending the Sunday School. Evening services for adults replaced afternoon meetings. Problems of intimidation by a number of ladies from the nearest Church of England Church were soon encountered. These ladies tried, with some success, to dissuade attendance. During 1886 the highest attendance was forty-five children and twenty-three adults.

By February 1886 plans for the new Chapel in **Feb** Woking were in an advanced state and in March it was **1886** reported that financial matters were also encouraging. In April, Trustees for the Church property were appointed including Henry William Gloster, Henry William Gloster (Junior) and Edward William Tarbox. In May, the members agreed to accept the lowest tender which was from Messrs Harris and Son (£1185) and by 11 August the official stone laying service was held; Enoch Moore and Edward William Tarbox laid the stones. After a public tea in the afternoon, an open meeting was held at the Wesleyan Chapel in Commercial Road. During the autumn a temporary loan was arranged with the bank to pay for some of the building work; as security the trust deeds for the Chapel were made available to the Bank.

Whilst building work was in progress, Mr Crewdson, responsible for the work at Knap Hill, offered his resignation. He claimed that he was unhappy with the public character of Edward William Tarbox. At a Special Church Meeting held on 14 November Mr Crewdson failed to substantiate his claims and as such was asked to make an apology. Members agreed that if an apology was not forthcoming, he would be honourably dismissed; as far as can be ascertained this apology was not forthcoming.

In Baptist Churches in Surrey (1909) it is recorded that "A pretty and convenient chapel was built and opened in 1886. This larger building, seating three hundred and thirty persons, was soon well filled and the cost of it was duly met at the time and the sum of £2000 covered the total outlay on land, school, vestries and chapel".

Two important matters were discussed at a Church **Dec** meeting held in December 1886. The first involved **1886** believer's baptism; should the person wishing to be baptised be immersed forwards or backwards. No decision was made at this time, the pastor was happy with either way. However, at an informal vote during February 1887 it was decided by nine votes to five to **Feb** adopt the forward method. The second subject was the **1887** observance of communion if the Pastor was away. It was agreed that an appointee could lead communion and anybody, who felt so disposed, could lead in prayer.

On 16 February 1887 J H Smith became a Christian at Woking with far-reaching results: He resolved to go and live among the people at Anthony's, build a larger mission room and become the resident manager. His desire was fulfilled and a new mission room seating one hundred was opened on 24 November 1887. By 1 January 1889 the services included singing classes, a young men's band, Bible class, Sunday School, needlework and clothing meetings and the aid of the poor.

It was decided to form a separate, but closely linked,

Church fellowship with J H Smith as the Pastor and this commenced on 24 March 1889. However, J H Smith left the locality in 1890 and Edward William Tarbox purchased the property and some adjoining cottages and acted as honorary pastor. After serving its purpose for fourteen years (1887 - 1901) the mission room became too small and the Pastor built a new chapel at his own expense, only asking the congregation to provide funds for working expenses. The new chapel was opened by Rev Charles Spurgeon in May 1901.

1887 Back in the middle of 1887 Edward William Tarbox announced that in his opinion "the time had arrived when we as a Church should take an interest in mission work in the 'foreign field'". Following a period of discussion, it was unanimously agreed that the fellowship would take a Sunday collection once a year for the general fund of the Baptist Missionary Society and a communion offering once yearly for the support of widows and orphans of missionaries. The Sunday School was also invited to support foreign missionary work.

On 11 September 1887 the first public baptisms were **Sep** held in the new building; eight people were baptised. **1887**

The efficient running of the Church was discussed during the early part of 1888 and it was agreed that the **1888** Deaconate should be enlarged and strengthened by the election of Elders. These Elders were to be appointed for a period of time (one, two, or three years) and then they would be eligible for re-election. Their duties were to co-operate with the Pastor on spiritual matters.

The Church was not without its difficulties. In late 1888 two serious issues, separate but closely interlinked, surfaced causing much concern amongst Church members. The first involved theology and the second a more personal matter. At the heart of the theological matter, called the "Down-Grade Controversy", was a challenge to the accepted view of the atonement and how the Surrey and Middlesex Baptist Association, the Baptist Union and the Church in Woking should respond. Henry William Gloster queried both the motives of the Surrey and Middlesex Baptist Association with what he called "pandering to Spurgeon" and how the Pastor had made a proposal for the Association to withdraw from the Baptist Union [Note: In a later clarification, the Pastor said that his call to break the ties with the Baptist Union was not related to the "Down-Grade Controversy" and that it referred to his concerns over too much centralisation of the Baptist Union].

The second issue discussed at the Church meeting involved Henry William Gloster's position within the Church. Comments had been received saying that the Church was held together by his personal influence and would not exist if he withdrew his support. Henry William Gloster said that he had considered the matter very seriously and he was of the opinion that for him to remain in a position of authority at the Church would hinder its spiritual blessing. Consequently, to demonstrate that this allegation was not true he tendered his resignation. Having stated his case, he shook hands with the Pastor and left the meeting.

Whilst the offer of resignation was not taken any further at the meeting, it was eventually accepted with much sorrow and regret. A new Treasurer was elected on 28 November 1888, but only on the proviso that he would step down if Henry William Gloster returned. **Nov 1888**

On 2 January 1889 the Church voted on the following motion raised by Mr Burrows "The Church withdraw from the Surrey and Middlesex Association in consequence of the recent circular excluding members from being delegates unless baptised, which is a departure from the Constitution under which the Church stood in our union with the Association". After making a statement to members, Edward William Tarbox said that he had made up his mind to let the motion pass unopposed. He continued that there had been a very strong difference of opinion between himself and Henry William Gloster with respect to the Association and now they had an opportunity of burying the disagreement in the resolution. He said that "not only would he refrain from opposition but would cheerfully and without grudging express his **Jan 1889** pleasure at being able to meet Mr Gloster's views". Following applause from those at the meeting Henry William Gloster expressed his pleasure at the handsome way in which the Pastor had spoken and acted.

Jan At a Special Church Meeting held on 4 January 1891
1891 the Pastor, Rev Tarbox, tended his resignation. He was of the opinion that the Church had not prospered for the previous two years and needed a Pastor who lived in the area. Whilst he had hoped to be able to come and live in Woking this had not been possible. His wife's health was another factor in his decision, as it prevented her from working in the Church. After eleven and a half years he felt that he had become a hindrance to the Church's prosperity. Members accepted his resignation, but only with much regret and Henry William Gloster closed the meeting in prayer. Edward William Tarbox preached his final sermon on Easter Sunday 29 March 1891.

CHAPTER 3

YEARS OF CHANGE

Pastors: John Owen 1891 to 1894; Ernest Judson Page 1895 to 1897; W Baldwin 1898 to 1900; AE Autram 1901 to 1904; Arthur Stanton 1905 to 1907; Willis Humphreys 1908 to 1910

On 8 April 1891 finance and the quest to find a new **Apr** Pastor were discussed at a Church meeting. With **1891** regard to finance it was announced that as at December 1890 expenditure had reached £360 3s 8d with receipts totalling only £249 10s 2d. There was also a debt resulting from the building of the Chapel of £396 2s 0d. Members agreed that from now on the

Church accounts should be formally published and also that Mr Gloster (unclear from the records which one) should be appointed as treasurer. With regard to identifying a new Pastor, Dan Gloster suggested, and it was agreed that John Owen, from Sunderland, should be invited to preach during May, with a view to taking on the position. At the end of May a Special Church Meeting was convened, and it was agreed to offer John Owen the position on a permanent basis, with an option for either the Church or him to terminate the arrangement at six months' notice. It was decided that he should be offered a salary of £100 plus any surplus (greater than £50) from the Church seat rental. He accepted the offer and commenced duties on 24 June 1891.

1891 In the early autumn of 1891 Mr Laker and Mr Gloster[2] proposed at a Church meeting that the Church should

---

[2] Unclear from the record which member of the Gloster family this was.

seek to purchase Farmville Villas in Goldsworth Road. Members unanimously agreed that the Deacons could spend up to £900 on the purchase. Unfortunately, the owner was unwilling to accept the offer and the matter was dropped. Subsequently Goldsworth Hall was rented for three months for Sunday afternoon services.

At the Annual General Meeting it was reported that at the end of December 1891 the Church had a balance at **Dec** the bank of £20 7s 6½d and that the average weekly **1891** offering during 1891 had been £2 2s 6d. There were sixty-eight members on the roll and the Sunday School was flourishing. On average sixty attended the Sunday morning service and eighty-seven in the afternoon. A Debt Extinction Scheme had been set up with the object of raising £400 by mid-summer to clear the Church of the building debt. It was noted that the "mutual improvement meetings" were proving very successful and were well attended (sixty-six people). At these meetings selected topics were discussed, including "the population of the villages", "the opium traffic", "theosophy", "Sunday opening of museums" and "the equality of the sexes". Attendees had also decided that "a republic would suit England better than a limited monarchy". Another strong point in the syllabus had been lectures on electricity, the chemistry of the dinner table and how a newspaper is made.

1892 In June and July it was agreed to draw up a Code of Rules for Church Government, set up a musical committee, increase the Pastor's salary to £125 per year, allow Church members to say the Lord's Prayer after the Pastor subject to review[3], rent the adjoining property for meetings during the week and as an infants' room on Sundays (rental £1 12s 6d per quarter-year).

The Church building fund debt remained at least until

---

[3] Following a trial period, it was decided not to continue with this practice.

October 1893 when it is recorded that Dan Gloster **Oct** encouraged members to clear the residue. He was of **1893** the opinion that if fifty people committed themselves to resolving the problem it would soon be written off. A number of members immediately pledged support and those present agreed to have a "thank offering". At the "thank offering" held on 1 January 1894, after a time of praise and an address from the Pastor, £50 was received towards the debt.

The Church continued to prosper and the need for additional accommodation re-surfaced. Consequently, in October 1894 the Church once again authorised the **Oct** Deacons to seek to purchase Farmville Villas for up to **1894** £850.

On 31 October John Owen, whose strength was failing, tendered his resignation. He and his doctors had decided that a move to South Africa may help. The Church accepted his resignation and his last day of service was on 10 November 1894. Unfortunately, the change of climate did not have the desired effect **Feb** and a cablegram was received to say that he had died **1895** on 19 February 1895.

The Church sought a replacement for John Owen and Mr Rowland Sturt was invited to take on the duties temporarily.

Apr At the Annual Church Meeting held on 3 April 1895 it **1895** was reported that during the past year, ten new members had joined the Church, bringing the membership total to eighty-two. Forty ladies regularly attended the Mothers' meeting and a relief fund was set up to help people cope with the severe winter weather; grocery, coal (a total of three tons), meat and soup were provided. At the same meeting the Treasurer reported that income for the year had been £482 6s 2½d.

Following several Church meetings in the spring of 1895 it was agreed to invite Ernest Judson Page to become the Pastor at a salary of £150 per year. He subsequently accepted the offer.

Problems with space continued and on 31 October 1895 it was agreed that the Sunday School needed more room. On 27 February 1896 it was decided to go **Feb** ahead with the purchase of Farmville Villas for £850 **1896** and on 1 April the following motion was passed: "Woking Baptist Congregational Church resolves to purchase the property adjoining Farmville Villas at the corner of Goldsworth Road and Percy Street". It was decided to erect a new Chapel on the land including classrooms and vestries. The present Chapel would be used for a School Hall and the work carried out in six sections, beginning with the classrooms (as soon as two thirds of the money for each section was guaranteed). The new Church would be known as "The Woking Free Church".

On 1 October the Church accepted the offer to rent **Oct** No1 Farmville Villas at a rent of £20 per annum, until **1896** the completion of the purchase. The upper rooms were sub-let to Mrs Bonsey who agreed to take on the

31

position of Chapel Keeper. Appendix D, Figure 2 shows a map of Woking in 1896.

Feb On 4 February 1897 the Trust Deed for the holding of
1897 Farmville Villas was unanimously agreed by the Church. However, progress with the legalities was very slow and it was decided to adjourn further decisions for three months. In the meantime, the front downstairs of No 1 Farmville Villas was used for weeknight meetings and as the Deacons' Vestry. In April 1897 the wisdom of delaying the building scheme until October was discussed; one of the reasons was that there were rumours of war in Turkey. However, one month later it was decided, by nine votes to two, to authorise the Trustees to complete the purchase of Farmville Villas by September and then hold the property on behalf of the Church.

Jun In June 1897 the Church took the unanimous decision
1897 to go forward with the building of Goldsworth Road Chapel (See Appendix D, Figure 7). It was looked upon as a "turning point with us in our Church life and

work". The Church would be based on "New Testament" principles and not associated directly with any denomination. At the same Church meeting the Pastor tendered his resignation "to heal divisions within his Church". At a Special Church Meeting, held on the next day (1 July 1897) when thirty-six members attended, his resignation was accepted, and it was agreed that his last Sunday would be 3 October.

During 1897 it was recorded that the Church had **Dec** dropped as low as twenty-eight active members, four **1897** associates and five honorary members with an average attendance at weekly meetings of twenty. Baptist Churches in Surrey (1909) described the period as "during which time the Church passed through many vicissitudes, and there was considerable loss".

From November 1897 to March 1898, Edward **Mar** William Tarbox came back to the pulpit at the request **1898** of the Church and during those five months he succeeded in restoring the congregation and putting things once more on a satisfactory footing (Baptist

Churches in Surrey, 1909).

Jun Activity to find a new Pastor commenced during the
1898 winter months but it was not until June 1898 that two
possible applicants (Revs Barnett and W Baldwin)
were considered at a Special Church Meeting. Voting
was initially split with W Baldwin receiving thirty-
four votes compared to thirteen for Rev Barnett (plus
two blanks). In a subsequent vote for W Baldwin
alone, the result was an almost unanimous agreement
to invite him to become Pastor. On 30 June W
Baldwin accepted the position.

At the beginning of September, it was agreed to obtain
estimates for lighting the Chapel with gas (£14 15s 0d)
and to construct a rail around the baptistery so that it
could be kept open.

Oct On 31 October 1898 the subject of raising a mortgage
1898 on the Church property to meet the new debt (£30)
was discussed. However, at the following Church
meeting it was decided to make a special effort to
raise at least £100 for the purpose of renovating the

Church, Sunday School room and repaying the building debt of £30. The Treasurer noted that it was costing £4 per week to fund the Church and currently the income was only just £4.

At the Annual General Meeting, held on 2 January **Jan** 1900 it was said that at the start of 1899 there had **1900** been ninety-six members, but only sixty-nine at the end of the year; one of the reasons behind the reduction in numbers was due to a strict analysis of attendance. On average thirty-nine people attended Sunday meetings. At the same meeting Henry William Gloster resigned his position as Treasurer and Deacon; this was accepted with much regret and much appreciation of his services over the years.

On 29 May 1900 W Baldwin resigned as Pastor on the **May** grounds of ill health. This was accepted. **1900**

The search for a replacement Pastor began straight **Feb** away, but it took until 28 February 1901 for the **1901** Church to invite Rev A E Autram to accept the role at a salary of £120 per year, with four Sunday's vacation.

35

In 1901 the average Sunday attendance was twenty-six in the morning and forty-nine in the afternoon, the Sunday School had sixty-nine children on its books. The Mothers' Meeting was very popular and had an average attendance of thirty-nine mothers out of a possible forty on the books.

May 1904 After three years of ministry, A E Autram, handed in his resignation on 27 May 1904. Clearly the situation had become difficult and there is mention of forming an alternative Baptist Church in Woking.

Jan 1905 The next Pastor, Arthur Stanton, was eventually invited to become Pastor in January 1905 and he commenced duties on 19 February. In April, forty members offered to pray for him for a three-month period.

1906 It was decided on 31 January 1906 that no renovation work would commence on the building without the Church having the finance in its hands.

At an evangelistic mission in May 1906 fourteen confessed to having found Christ; the meetings were so popular that they were extended by four days.

On 28 November 1906 Arthur Stanton informed members, to their great surprise, that he had been invited to become the Pastor at a Church in Southend and that he was carefully considering the request. On the following Sunday at the evening service he told attendees that he had declined the offer from Southend as he believed that there was still a great work to be done in Woking.

In the report of activity for 1906, at which ninety-five were present, questions were asked concerning how all of those wishing to attend Sunday services could be fitted into the existing accommodation. During the year thirty-nine had joined the Church (nineteen by profession of faith and twenty by transfer), the average morning attendance was thirty-one with sixty-six at evening communion. There was also a need for a Church vestry. One interesting event had taken place during the year and that was that the Pastor had taken a special mission at Newhaven and returned home with a bride!

In April 1907 it was agreed to hold four united services with other local Churches, led by various **May** ministers and on 28 May 1907 it was reported that **1907** Henry William Gloster had become seriously ill; the Church wrote to him and his wife expressing their sympathies.

Chapel renovation work costing £20 was completed in the summer of 1907. A report said that the Chapel "looked beautiful".

During the late summer and autumn there was discussion concerning the provision of heating and ventilation for the Church; this was estimated to cost around £100. Could the work start before the money was available? Should the heating consist of radiators or pipes? In November it was proposed and agreed that, given the exceptional circumstances, work costing £168 7s 5d could proceed. Funding of the work remained a concern as at that time the Church only had £70. It was decided to approach the bank and seek a loan against the deeds of the Church.

On 6 October 1907 a letter of resignation from the Pastor, Arthur Stanton, was received and accepted with regret. He had been invited by London Road Baptist Church, Portsmouth to become their minister. Baptist Churches in Surrey (1909) summarised his ministry as "very successful".

At the same meeting in October it was proposed that "nobody would be eligible for office in the Church if they drank intoxicating drink". Following discussion on the merits or otherwise of drink the motion was lost by thirty to fourteen votes.

1908 began with a call for prayer concerning the **1908** appointment of the next Pastor. The Deacons recommended that Willis Humphreys should be invited at a salary of £150 per year. In a ballot which required a two thirds majority, all members expressed their agreement with the proposal. He agreed to the appointment, took up office on 29 March 1908 and was officially welcomed at a social gathering on 1

April 1908. Members discussed how best to offset the Pastor's reduced income as a result of moving to Woking; this included giving him the rent and paying the rates for his house in York Road or by taking a special collection.

Apr At a members' meeting in April 1908 the sad news of
1908 the death followed by interment at Brookwood Cemetery of Henry William Gloster on 7 April was announced. The Church decided to make a permanent memorial to him in recognition of his service since the Church's foundation. A memorial tablet was subsequently erected to acknowledge Henry William Gloster's service (11 November 1920).

1909 During the first half of 1909 there was considerable discussion concerning communion and in particular whether individual cups should be used for the wine. There were strong arguments on either side, with one group concerned about the transmission of diseases such as consumption and influenza. The matter was resolved at a Church meeting held on 27 July 1909 when thirty-nine people attended (seventeen men and twenty-two women). Sixteen voted for individual cups, eight were against and two ballot papers were returned blank. The cost of communion trays and eighty cups was estimated to be around £4. It was agreed to purchase ninety-six cups and start the new system in the New Year. Communion glasses were placed on every other seat to prevent accidents.

During 1908 and 1909 the Church's financial position was not in good shape. For example, there was a negative balance on the renovation fund of £70 which had been borrowed from the bank (November 1908). In July 1909 the Treasurer reported that the Church owed £27 and only had £5 14s 8d to meet its debt. By March 1910 problems with finances had worsened **Mar** with Sunday offerings becoming smaller. It was **1910** estimated that if the trend continued the Church would have a debt of £40 by the end of the year. Additionally, the Pastor, who was very gracious about the matter, said that he believed that he needed £200 a year to live in Woking; prayer was recommended by the Pastor. One consequence of the poor financial position was that there was no money to buy hymn books for any visitors; Church members were asked to pay 5s each for their own books. Two concerts were organised with a view to purchasing the much-needed hymn books from the proceeds.

On 26 October the resignation of Willis Humphreys was announced to Church members and it was agreed to his release from 20 November.

CHAPTER 4

GROWTH AND THE GREAT WAR

Pastor: Harold Tebbit 1911 - 1919

The search for a new Pastor commenced once again. Two main candidates were forthcoming. The first was Rev Owen (from Fleet) and the second Harold Tebbit. By February 1911 Harold Tebbit had preached five **Feb** times, each time with a rising number of attendees; **1911** eighty-four (the highest for some years) were present at evening communion in February. Younger members were particularly drawn to him. Three tests for appointment of a pastor were agreed:

- Does he hold the great essential truths of

Christianity?

- Does he have a gift of presenting the truth?
- Does he help members engage more perfectly in the work to which God has called us?

Apr 1911

It was decided unanimously by the forty members present to invite Harold Tebbit to become Pastor at a salary of £110 per year and to commence his ministry on 2 April 1911.

Feb 1912

The following three brief insights into Church life were extracted from the records. Firstly, during the autumn of 1911 there was considerable debate concerning the merit and consequences of purchasing a new organ. Eventually it was agreed to purchase one from Hastings for £195. Secondly Harold Tebbit and his wife sat in the vestry on New Year's Day and members were invited to pay them a visit and exchange greetings and thirdly in February 1912 it was decided to hold a special mission during March with the aim of deepening the spiritual life of the Church and helping others who were seeking a

Saviour.

Evangelism took on a new dimension with the formation of a cycling club, under the leadership of Mr Hickford. The objective was for members to cycle to nearby villages during the summer months and hold open air services.

A map of the area surrounding the Church, produced in 1912, is given at Appendix D, Figure 3. Much of the area surrounding the Church had been developed and it is probable that Farmville Villas, mentioned earlier, are the properties immediately adjacent to the Church.

The overall financial position of the Church improved during 1913. It was recorded on 6 August that there **Aug** was a positive balance of £31 7s 9½d. Numbers of **1913** active communion members had also increased to one hundred and thirty-three with an additional thirty honorary members. Space in the building for Sunday worship was also causing difficulties and resulted in the resignation of one of the sidesmen (Mr Lush). He said that "owing to the large number of seats taken it was increasingly becoming difficult to find room for **May** visitors". At the following month's Church meeting it **1914** was agreed that all seat holders had to be in place five minutes before the start of a service and that no seat would be retained except by previous request to the stewards. Where visitors should sit was also discussed and it was suggested the first three seats close to the pulpit should be allocated to them. A decision on this was adjourned until June. In June an alternative amendment to this suggestion was considered and it was proposed to allocate twenty seats in various parts of the building for visitors. On discussion it was decided to delay any decision for six months.

During May, Harold Tebbit's salary was discussed by members. It was proposed to increase it to £130 plus any surplus after the Church's other expenditure had been met. Some thought that this was a step lacking in faith and proposed that the salary should be raised to £150; this motion was lost. A compromise was finally agreed where individual members were invited to make up the difference between £130 and £150.

The merit of using the Baptist Church Hymnal, rather than Psalms and Hymns, was discussed and whether these should be purchased from Church funds. It was decided to form a committee to investigate the matter. In September 1914 it was recommended that "the war **Sep** had altered the whole aspect of the question and that **1914** no decision should be made until after it had ended". However, it was felt that the matter could not wait that long and some hymn books were needed straight away; these were purchased with funds borrowed from the Church repair fund. The new books were used for the first time on the first Sunday in 1915.

The Great War had a big impact on Church life. Some members enlisted in military service and others remained in Woking. The names of those who subsequently died whilst on active service were listed on a memorial plaque mounted for all to see and remember on the Church wall. Appendix A gives detailed information about each of these brave men who served their country. A number of other war related stories are included in the following pages.

To help serve the soldiers it was decided to give them the fruit from the Harvest Festival service rather than to sell it. It was also decided to open the Sunday School room for them for reading, writing and refreshments.

It was agreed in November to write to the local military commander to see if it would be helpful to offer Christmas entertainment to the troops under his command. This was gratefully accepted, and Mr and Mrs Harvey entertained the troops at the Church, with the Deacons' wives taking turns at the refreshments' bar.

1914 The active membership roll in October 1914 was one hundred and fifty-two. In view of the steady progress **Mar** of the Church it was agreed to raise Harold Tebbit's **1915** salary to £150 in March 1915.

Harold Tebbit was made an official Chaplain at the Barracks in June 1915.

During the autumn of 1915 the possible installation of electric light in the Church was discussed; the cost being £30. There was some opposition to this proposal and a decision was deferred until the next meeting. However, it was then agreed to proceed. Another matter was raised at a Church meeting and that was whether the Church was insured against Zeppelin raids and it was established that it was.

Members from the Church were actively involved in the war and it was decided to send a small present to all who had joined the army. The sum of £3 12s 0d was raised by members. The sad news of the death of Edwin Reed, a gunner in the army, was received on 5 April 1916; he had died from wounds received on the **Apr** battlefield on 8 March. **1916**

On 27 September 1916 the active Church roll was one hundred and sixty-four; with an overall total of one hundred and ninety (no increase during the year) and on 17 January the Church held a balance of £13 18s 11d, with a yearly revenue of £261 0s 2d. Harold

Tebbit's salary was increased by £25.

Feb In February 1917 Harold Tebbit was approached by
1917 the YMCA and invited to spend four months with the
soldiers in France. This matter was discussed at a
Special Church Meeting and his release, on full salary,
was approved. After problems obtaining a Home
Office pass to go to France he finally went in the
summer of 1917 and returned safely in October.

May In May 1917 it was reported that two Snell brothers
1917 had been killed in the war.

The Church organist and choirmaster for sixteen
years, Mr Gilbert Macdonald, offered his resignation,
as he was joining the army. His resignation was not
accepted, and he was given temporary leave of
absence. Subsequently it was confirmed that he had
died on 28 November 1917.

Oct In October 1917 the grand total of members had risen
1917 to one hundred and ninety-five; this was five more
than the previous year.

It was decided on 24 October 1917, that soldiers

should be sent Christmas parcels; the ladies of the Church were invited to knit garments with wool provided by the Church.

In February 1918 a letter was received from the **Feb** YMCA requesting that Harold Tebbit should return **1918** for special work with the army in France. The request was supported by members, when one hundred and twenty-two voted for the motion, with only two against. He returned from this work in May 1918.

Overall during the war fourteen members died in action: C Bessant, C Evitt, W G Fletcher, H Gloster, S W Hayter, P Holder, H Jater, G P Macdonald, D W Orr, A Provins, H Provins, E Reed, H Snell and N Snell. (See memorial boards in Appendix D Figure 12.)

The total Church roll during the autumn of 1918 was two hundred and four.

The matter of Church accommodation, particularly for the Sunday School work, re-surfaced in September **Sep** 1918. It was agreed to purchase four cottages and land **1918** at the rear of the existing Church building in Percy Street (now known as Victoria Way) for £750. Funding for the purchase of the houses was delayed until the following month when it was agreed to have an appeal for gifts and loans for the purchase of the cottages and land. It was also agreed to appoint a twelve member "Forward Movement Committee", the terms of which were to:

- Manage the property in Percy Street until such a time as the proposed buildings could be erected on the site.

- Consider schemes for raising the money to pay for the property, build a Sunday School and institute.

- Decide when it was right to go ahead with the building work.

- Invite an architect to design and builders to tender for the building work.

- Appoint their own officers to form subcommittees.

- Submit to the Deaconate their schemes for raising money.

Negotiations on obtaining the right of way between the existing Church premises and the new property commenced straight away and were finally agreed in December.

On 27 October 1918 Harold Tebbit, the Pastor, **Oct** informed members that he had been invited to become **1918** the Pastor at Teddington. He hoped that the "Forward Movement" would flourish. Following a tribute to the Pastor it was agreed to write to him and urge him not to leave. As an incentive it was agreed to increase his salary to £200 with a bonus of £25 straight away. However, this encouragement was not successful, and he submitted his written resignation to the Church on 15 December 1918 and a farewell service was held on 16 February 1919.

Church finances were reported to be in a healthy **Jan** position in January 1919 and it was agreed to transfer **1919** £70 to the "Forward Movement". By March it was recorded that weekly giving would soon enable the outstanding balance on the purchase of the cottages to be cleared.

CHAPTER 5

A NEW BUILDING, GROWTH AND ANOTHER WORLD WAR

Pastor: Middleton Price 1920 to 1934; Stanley
Harrison 1934 to 1944

On 14 May 1919 questions were asked about the **May** progress of finding a replacement for Harold Tebbit. A **1919** number of people had preached on a Sunday, but were any suitable to be invited to preach "with a view of becoming the Pastor"? Names of four applicants were written down on the blackboard and a vote for each was taken. Out of the thirty-nine members present twenty-two thought that Rev Evans was a distinct possibility. As a consequence, it was decided to invite Rev Evans from Wrexham to another Sunday service. At the same meeting it was announced that, following the death of Rev Tarbox sometime earlier, Mrs Tarbox offered, as a gift, the premises at Anthony's. This was accepted.

It would appear that the Church decided not to invite Rev Evans to become the pastor and instead they invited Rev Newell from Taunton to preach and subsequently to become the Pastor; it was decided to offer him £230 plus any balance which was over at the end of the year. Rev Newell turned this offer down and said that he would not accept anything less than £250. The Church decided not to pursue the matter any further.

Oct In October 1919 it was decided to invite Rev **1919** Maishman to preach for a second time. Following this visit it was decided to offer him the position. However, he declined the offer having already accepted the "call" from a Church in Yorkshire.

Middleton Price, from Dulwich, was subsequently **1920** invited to preach and then by a massive majority of forty-two to one, invited to become the Pastor at a salary of £250 plus any balance left over at the end of the year. The congregation at a Sunday service were asked to vote on the matter. This clearly went favourably, and it was agreed that his ministry should commence on 8 February 1920.

On 23 March 1920 the Church formally took on the **1920** responsibility for Anthony's and formed a committee to help run it. It was also decided at the same meeting to erect a special memorial tablet to those who had died during the Great War.

In April 1920 the "Forward Movement" sought **Apr** authority to acquire seven cottages/shops, belonging to **1920** Mr Crane, adjoining the Percy Street cottages for up to £800. This was approved and in July it was agreed to go ahead with the purchase at £1300.

By September 1920 the contract for the purchase of **Sep** the cottages/shops was signed and a mortgage agreed. **1920**

Rough plans for a new Sunday School room were shown to members and provisionally approved.

The Church had been renting a hut in Oriental Road for the use of the Church Scout Group. It was decided to build a new hut behind two of the shops for the use of the Scouts and the Sunday School. The new facility was called the Baptist Church Institute and was **Oct** opened by Mrs Henry William Gloster on 31 October **1921** 1921.

Mar On 15 March 1923 it was reported that after an **1923** alternative site for a new Church had failed to be approved, the advice from the architects was to pull down four of the cottages and build on the land. Rough sketch plans had been drawn up and put out to tender. In June 1923 a letter was written to Woking Council offering to sell them some of the existing Church land in Goldsworth Road for use as a library and in the same month plans for the new building were approved by the local authority. However, no decision had been heard from the local authority concerning the purchase of the surplus land for a library. In July 1923 it was reported that a piece of land was given to the Church by the Friary Brewery.

On 1 November 1923 at a Church meeting at which **Nov** forty-five members were present, it was reported that **1923** the local authority was unlikely to purchase the additional land for a library and that it had been decided to sell the premises through an agent. With regard to the new building it was agreed that Messrs Nomes would be asked to start building work immediately at a cost of £9236. At the end of the month it was reported that an overdraft at 1% above base rate, not exceeding £7000 had been agreed with the bank; the deeds of the property were to be held by the Baptist Union and Davies the solicitor.

Away from the Church building project two significant changes were agreed. Firstly, members could be excluded from the Church if they did not attend the Lord's Supper or Sunday services. Those who failed to attend would be subject to an inquiry by the Pastor and if there was not a good reason for their absence, they would be removed. Secondly, nine Deacons would be elected, each to serve for a three-year period.

Apr 1924 On 30 April 1924 the official stone laying ceremony took place. Percy Street was closed "joyfully" by the Roman Catholic Priest. At the ceremony, conducted by Rev J C Carlisle, President of the Baptist Union, stones were laid by Mrs Tarbox, Mrs H W Gloster, H Marnham (treasurer and ex-president of the Baptist Union) and H O Serpell J. P. High Sherriff of Surrey. They were actually re-laying the stones that had been laid on 10 February 1880 in the first Church building by the late Rev E W Tarbox and the late Mr H W Gloster.

After the ceremony there was a public tea in the Wesleyan Lecture Hall, an organ recital and a public meeting (in the Wesleyan Church). At the public meeting the hymn "The Church's one foundation is Jesus Christ her Lord" was sung. On the back of the order of service there was an artist's impression of what the Church would eventually look like and a tear off slip inviting contributions to the building fund (see Appendix D, Figures 8 and 9). Figure 10 shows a sketch by Chas Davis of what the building actually looked like from the time that it was built until the Church moved to its next site in 1976. There is also a photograph of the Percy Street building (Figure 11).

On 30 October 1924, when fifty-five Church members **Oct** were present, the disposal of the old Church buildings **1924** was discussed. Consideration was given to leasing the property over twenty-one years at an annual rent of £250. There was an additional purchase clause of a buyer paying a lump sum of £3500. The possibility of selling the property to Woking Council for use as a library was once again discussed. A month later a reply from Woking Council was received saying that they could not see the way to arranging the purchase of the old buildings for a new library. However, interest had been received through an Estate Agent. Church members discussed their preferred method being the sale of the premises as one process, although the possibility of taking a first stage payment of £500 with the remainder spread over a number of years was an alternative. Interest at 2% above bank rate would also be charged. The meeting was adjourned without taking any final decision on the matter. However, later that month (November 1924) it was agreed to go ahead.

Jan 1925 The possible opening of the new Church on 14 January 1925 was discussed by members and £500 set aside for the erection of the Church organ. (Church music has played a significant role in the development of the Church over the years. Tony Lyttle traces the use of music and song in the worship of the congregation in Appendix B, from John Gloster's historic records and from more contemporary notes provided by Alice Potter, widow of Barry Potter who was the Church organist at Percy Street from the early 1950s to 1976 and then pianist, along with Alice, too, at The Coign until he retired around about 2000.)

Unfortunately, it was reported in December that discussions over the sale of the old building had fallen through. It was not all bad news, though, as by April the Church had purchased a strip of land from Woking Urban District Council for £100.

In August 1925 an offer of rental (£250 p.a.) was **Aug** received for the old premises. It was proposed that the **1925** building would be used for a "dance hall". This offer was turned down as it was believed that this use was not acceptable. A more acceptable rental offer was subsequently received in October 1925 from R & S Colman, although final details appeared not to be settled for some months to come. To help finance the new Church building a temporary loan from the Baptist Union was sought and obtained.

In the 1925 accounts it was stated that the Church had £588 17s 7d in the general account. The Church was not consumed with plans for expansion, and evangelism continued with the distribution of tracts and in September the possibility of showing the film

"Life of Livingstone" at the local cinema was discussed. By the following June it was agreed to set up a Pastoral Committee to help the Pastor discharge

Jul his duties. In July 1926 it was agreed that the Church
1926 should sell the cottages in Russell Road, Horsell, as they were not a paying proposition[4]; these were eventually sold for £550 in April 1929. In November the Church produced an edition of "Forward Magazine", a free, eight-page booklet. 500 copies were produced and distributed widely. (Appendix D, Figures 13-15 show 1924, '31 and '37 editions.)

1927 On 25 January 1927 it was reported at a Church meeting that there was £813 in the Church account and £53 11s 1d in the Benevolent Fund. By September Brownies, Girl Guides and Scouts were doing well at the Church. It was also decided to increase the

---

[4] How or when these cottages became Church property is unclear from the records.

Pastor's salary, but this was made conditional on an increase in general giving. One new initiative was the setting up of the Bureau of Services, at which advice on finance and legal matters could be provided to those in need.

In the spring of 1928 the possibility of funding a trip **1928** for the Pastor, Rev Middleton Price, to Toronto was discussed and Mr Serpell (High Sheriff of Surrey and Church member) kindly donated £500. The Church was also involved in matters outside its own local sphere; it voted against the amendments to the Prayer Book which were before the Houses of Parliament and passed a resolution to curtail alcoholic drinks at sports meetings.

Whilst the Church was still progressing, there remained a debt on the Church building. This was discussed on several occasions and Mr Serpell generously gave £1000 to help. The Church was asked to provide preachers at Pirbright for twelve months. Another Forward Magazine was published in

Dec December 1928, the subject being "how to write off
1928 debt".

Church planting continued when an opportunity to purchase "House Field" in Kingfield, South Woking arose. Mr Serpell once again helped financially. By
Feb February 1929 the purchase had been completed and
1929 in April an architect was appointed to prepare plans for the new Kingfield Church. Whilst a temporary hold-up with the new building was reported in June, it was decided to go ahead with the arrangement of services.

Jul The work officially commenced on 7 July 1929, with
1929 Sunday services and a Sunday School being held in a tent; an organ was obtained to provide the music. The possibility of having electric light and water in the tent was discussed. At the same time, it was reported that building plans were submitted to the Council and were approved in early autumn 1929. Students from Spurgeon's Bible College provided support to the work and this started to flourish over the coming

months.

Permission for a second wooden building in which the Sunday School could meet was obtained and a tender of £1687 for the work accepted. The official stone laying ceremony at Kingfield took place on 30 November 1929 and the opening ceremony during March 1930.

The work at Pirbright continued and six from the Church in Pirbright became members of the Woking Church. Membership at both Pirbright and Kingfield was through the main Church at Woking.

By July 1930 it was reported that the Church at **July** Kingfield had twenty-five members and a student **1930** pastor, Mr Missen, who had helped right from the start of the work was appointed at £1 10s per week; he officially took on his new responsibilities in September 1930.

The main Church in Woking was actively involved with Woking Urban District Council. An extract from correspondence written at the time described one

Oct
1930 particular event "On Saturday 25 October 1930 at the Woking Council Chambers, Mr H O Serpell and his cousin Miss Oliver entertained members and officials of the Council. Mr H O Serpell presented Mr Quartermaine, the Chairman of Woking Urban District Council, a document of authority for the use of an ensign of arms of the town. At the same time, he invested Mr Quartermaine with a handsome robe, a gold badge and chain of office to be worn by successive Chairman of the Council". The Church was also involved in other local matters including objecting to the opening of a cinema in Woking.

For many years Communion cards had been issued to Church members but this practice ceased in the summer of 1931. At the same time a library was started at the Church and was run by a committee consisting of thirteen people.

Sep
1931 In September 1931 it is reported that Mr Missen's time at Kingfield had come to an end; he was required to concentrate on his 4th year studies at university. The

work was taken over by Mr Battson.

Evangelism continued during 1931 when the Church minutes record that a "Young life week" had been organised. This was clearly successful, and it was noted that, during the week, four had become Christians.

During 1932 and 1933 the links between Woking **1932** Urban District Council and the Church became even more established and Civic Services were held at the Church in Percy Street in the month of April in 1932 and in 1933.

Towards the end of 1933 it is recorded that the work at **1933** Kingfield was expanding; there was now a Women's Own group, Young Women's Bible classes, a monthly members' meeting and a choirmaster had been appointed.

In January 1934 it was decided to hold a mission at **Jan** Percy Street. Prayer, advertising and handbills (three **1934** thousand) were all prepared and the mission advertised in the Woking News and Mail.

Also, in January Middleton Price, the Pastor, tendered his resignation as he had been invited to a Church in **Mar** Fulham. His last service was on 18 March 1934. The **1934** Church had definitely flourished under his Pastorate; when he left there were just over three hundred and fifty active Church members. Also, the work at Anthony's was continuing and in 1934 celebrated its 49th anniversary.

A map of the area surrounding the Church is shown in Appendix D, Figure 4. The location of the Church building in Percy Street (now Victoria Way) can be identified in the middle of the map.

Apr The search for a new Pastor started in April 1934 with **1934** the appointment of an Enquiry Committee. After a number of false starts it was agreed to send a deputation to Whitstable Baptist Church to hear Stanley Harrison. In July 1934 he was invited to become the Pastor (forty-six for, ten against). This invitation was accepted, and he started work on 1 December 1934.

Discussions took place in February and March 1935 **Feb**
about the need for an assistant Pastor at Kingfield. **1935**
One of the qualifications was that the person should
preferably be married or about to be. Rev Fredrick
Dimmick was appointed at a salary of £250 per year
and he started work on 1 August 1935.

In April 1935 it was decided to write a letter of
opposition to the opening of the swimming pool (in
Woking Park) on Sundays and in July it was decided
to reduce the number of notices made during a Sunday
service. Overall this did not work, and full notices
were restored in September 1935. Communion cards
were also reintroduced in October 1935.

In February 1936 the first "Welcome pack" for **Feb**
visitors was introduced. **1936**

The Church continued to expand at Kingfield during
1936 with membership reaching forty-nine. This
resulted in the need for further building work. By
November it was agreed to approach the Baptist
Union Forward Movement for further funding for the

work at Kingfield; Percy Street Church had spent £3000 in opening the Church, which was in an area of greater than five thousand people. The opening **Mar** ceremony for a new Kingfield Hall was set for 17 **1937** March 1937. Rev Dimmick agreed to continue in his work without a specified end date.

The work in Anthony's also continued to progress with three new scholars being added to the school. Similarly, at Pirbright the Sunday School was well attended. However, attendance at the evening services at Pirbright had become unsatisfactory and **Sep** deteriorated even more by September 1938. Despite **1938** this, members were prepared to carry on. Part of the problem at Pirbright was that a number of groups appear to have been involved and this had caused some difficulties e.g. Surrey Congregation Mission.

1939 By autumn 1939 the effects of the start of the Second World War were beginning to be noted in the Church minutes. For example, a discussion was held concerning opening the school room to receive children who had been evacuated from London and Evening Church meetings were not held between July 1939 and February 1940 as there was a need for the building to be fitted with blackout curtains.

In the Church accounts for 1939 it is recorded that a rent of £250 had been received for the old Church premises and £337 12s 0d rent from the cottages on the land where the Church would, it was hoped, be extended. However, the overall liability at the bank stood at £3653 8s 9d. Mr Ashley, an active Church member, became the Vice Chairman of Woking District Council. How to reach the men in the forces with the gospel was discussed and it was decided to hold a special service for them in the evening.

In September 1941 it is reported that the work at **Sep** Kingfield continued, four local Deacons had been **1941** appointed to conduct local administrative matters and, by November 1942, there were ninety-six scholars in the Sunday School. There was some slightly better news from Pirbright when the building in which the

May
1943
Church met was re-opened after two- or three-months' closure. However, the hall was requisitioned by the military in May 1943 and the work was closed down.

The Pastor spoke at the Civic Service on 9 May 1943 at the invitation of the Chairman Ashley Cook MBE. On 11 May 1943 it is recorded that Rev Dimmick, the Pastor, had handed in his notice at Kingfield as he had been invited to a Church in Lyndhurst, New Forest. The Church debt at Percy Street was gradually being reduced, but it still remained at over £2500; the situation was helped a little when the Bank Rate for the period of the war was reduced to 3.5%.

During 1943 there were discussions between the Churches in Woking concerning the degree of co-operation which could be achieved between the Roman Catholics and other Churches. The Catholics were of the opinion that they were not willing to co-operate on spiritual matters but were willing to work together on social matters.

The Kingfield Pastorate proved hard to fill as there

were one hundred and fifty Baptist ministers in the three armed services and most of the training colleges had been closed as a result of the war. Despite these difficulties, Rev Horton, who was very keen on "aggressive evangelism", finally agreed to take on the work. Rev Dimmick's farewell service was held on 11 August 1943. **Aug 1943**

The debt at Percy Street had been further reduced by January 1944 and it was agreed to ask the Baptist Union to make a ten-year loan of £2400; the loan being secured by a number of guarantees. At the same time it was decided to pass to the Baptist Union the deeds for the remaining properties. **Jan 1944**

On 20 June 1944, Rev Stanley Harrison tendered his resignation. In his letter he said that he felt that it was now the right time for him to go to Sudbury (Suffolk) after ten years in ministry at Woking. "When war came, he felt that it was his duty to stay, but the strain had taken its toll. He had been glad to open his house to the forces in Woking." **Jun 1944**

During the Second World War four Church members died in action (Douglas Allen, David Dimmick, Hamish Macdonald and Peter Rowe.)

CHAPTER 6

POST WAR YEARS

Pastor: Leslie Fraser 1945 to 1958

The process of selecting the new Pastor started immediately with the appointment of a seven-person committee. Three requirements for the new minister were defined - he should be a:

- Faithful Christian witness in the town.
- Soul winner.
- Soul builder.

Leslie Fraser was invited to preach on two occasions **Jan** and at a Special Church Meeting held on 28 January **1945**

1945, fifty-one out of a possible sixty attendees decided to invite him to become the Percy Street Pastor. He accepted the offer and agreed to start on 4 March.

By the end of January 1945, the Church debt had been reduced to under £2000. It is noted that the Church contacted the Surrey Public Control of Licensing Authority to say that attendance of under sixteens at the Sunday cinema should not be permitted; rather the authorities should be encouraging attendance at Sunday School. On 23 April 1945 it was agreed that the sideman would close the doors when the Pastor entered; this would ensure that the services commenced in a spirit of worship. In addition, it was agreed to re-form the choir to make it a "Christian choir".

Mar Work at both Anthony's and Kingfield continued and
1945 in March 1945 thirty to thirty-five attended the annual fellowship at Anthony's. It was decided that Kingfield would seek financial independence from the

Percy Street Church. However, before this could go ahead an increase in giving of £1 6s 0d per week was required.

With the end of the Second World War it was agreed to make the returning troops welcome at the Church. To help these, members would:

- Maintain a library with good literature.
- Welcome the troops into members' homes.
- Hold meetings after the Sunday services for discussion and singing.
- Provide a canteen.
- Send parcels to those who remained in the field.
- "Adopt a man or girl" on their return.

In March 1946 how best to encourage attendance at **Mar** Sunday evening services was discussed by members. **1946** It was pointed out that the Church was essentially a missionary organisation. Three approaches were proposed:

- Identify those who used to attend and encourage them to return.
- Each member should name one person and try and win them for the Lord.
- A group of "fishers" (with leaflets and tracts) would go out for about thirty minutes before a Sunday service and invite people to attend.

Apr 1946 Discussions took place in April 1946 concerning how best to extinguish the remaining Church building debt. It was proposed to sell off some properties in Church Street and by 28 January 1947 it was agreed to sell the seven cottages in Church Street (now known as Church Street West). At the same meeting it was agreed to create a memorial to those who had given their lives for their country in the Second World War.

Jul 1947 The memorial tablet was unveiled by Stanley Harrison on 6 July 1947. (See memorial boards in Appendix D, Figure 12.)

The work at Kingfield continued to expand and it was agreed that new premises were required for Sunday

School and youth work; the total cost for the work of building a sixty by thirty feet building, with a corrugated roof and steel window frames was estimated at £750. Percy Street agreed to loan the money on the condition that it was paid back at a rate of £100 per year. The building work of the new youth centre at Kingfield started during the autumn of 1947.

In September 1947 the Girls' Life Brigade was started **Sep** at Percy Street and it was hoped to form a Boys' **1947** Brigade company in the near future. It was decided that during the winter months the Church would hold a youth service, with community hymn signing and testimonies.

On 27 January 1948 it was announced that the Church **Jan** building debt had finally been cleared. **1948**

It was reported in January 1948 that, as there were only two locals who attended Sunday afternoon services at Anthony's, it had been decided to cease holding the service; however, with seventeen scholars, the Sunday School would continue.

A serious issue arose during the spring of 1948; a number of ladies had attended services without wearing a hat. Some members thought that this was unscriptural. The matter was referred to the Deacons, but no action appeared to be forthcoming.

1948 The new youth centre at Kingfield was opened during the spring of 1948 and it is recorded that the Girls Life Brigade had fifty members, the Boys Brigade twenty and the Sunday School over one hundred and twenty children. As a comparison during 1948, the Percy Street Sunday School had fifty-seven children on its books, an increase of twelve over the previous year.

Unfortunately, the resignation was received during April 1949 from Rev Perry Horton at Kingfield; the reason behind his decision was medical. The search for a new pastor was commenced and Rev G W Yaxley was invited to fill the vacancy in November 1949.

1950 At the start of 1950 the appointment of Elders to assist the Pastor at Percy Street with the spiritual welfare of the Church was discussed and Victor Rowe and Gilbert Simmons were mentioned as possible candidates. After a few months' consideration they were both appointed for an initial period of one year.

At the Annual General Meeting, held on 30 January **Jan** 1951, Leslie Gloster presented the accounts. **1951** Following acceptance there was a discussion on how best to present financial information to members. It was agreed that in future:

- The accounts would be provided in greater detail.
- They would be distributed to members before the meeting.

At the same meeting the office of Eldership was reviewed, and it was decided to carry on with the role for another twelve months. A 100% success rate had been achieved by Sunday School students who had entered the Scripture Examination.

Two main subjects took up members' time during the

1952 autumn of 1951 and early 1952. The first involved a major review of the Church Roll – it appears that following the exercise there were sixty-seven on the active list. Secondly, the financing of Kingfield; the objective being to make them self-sufficient. Income was £328, outgoings £610, with the remainder being provided by Percy Street. The possibility of applying for a bursary from the Baptist Union Homework Fund was discussed.

The development of Sheerwater Estate raised new opportunities for Percy Street members, and it was decided that the next Quarterly Church Magazine should contain a special welcome to the new people followed by a visit from Church members; two thirds of the visits were completed by April 1952.

The Church accounts for 1951 showed that Percy Street had an income of £2276 8s 4d.

Jul On 22 July 1952 it is recorded that a questionnaire
1952 concerning the prayer life of the Church had been circulated to members and an analysis of the data was

in progress. A grant from the Baptist Union had been agreed for Kingfield. With regard to spiritual progress four objectives were agreed:

- To raise weekly offerings to £20 per week (an increase £3 per week).
- To raise membership to its former level (this would mean adding seventy during 1952 - to date eight had been baptised, eleven come into membership and the Pastor was in touch with another ten).
- To double the evening congregation.
- "Each one to reach one".

By October 1952 the questionnaires concerning the **Oct** prayer life of the Church had been analysed and there **1952** was a preference to hold a prayer meeting at 19:30 on a Thursday evening.

At the end of 1952 the Rev G W Yaxley resigned from Kingfield on the taking up of an appointment at Yarmouth. After some months, David Boon was

Aug 1953 offered the position at Kingfield – he accepted, taking up duties on 1 August 1953.

At Percy Street, children were expected to sit with their parents during the Sunday morning service, with their own Sunday School taking place in the **Feb 1953** afternoon. However, in February 1953 it was agreed that children, under ten, should leave before the sermon and go to the Sunday School room for a talk of their own.

Jan 1954 It was decided in January 1954 that Deacons would assist the Pastor in visiting members in their homes as they felt that they would become more quickly aware of members in need. At the same meeting, members were informed that Stanley Harrison (the previous pastor) and his wife would retire back to Woking and wished to resume occupation of their property in Horsell which was currently being used by Leslie Fraser. To facilitate this arrangement the Deacons proposed that the Church would purchase a house for use as a manse.

Following an initial approach, in January 1954, to sell the old Church land in Goldsworth Road and a subsequent offer in the spring of 1954, members discussed the matter at a Special Church Meeting in May 1954. The Deacons thought that it was in the best **May** interest of the Church to sell the land. Whilst it was **1954** not possible to discuss the details of the offer it was expected to be around £10,000. The Secretary said that in his opinion the offer had come at just the right time with the decision to build the new manse. However, at this time members decided not to go ahead with the offer.

In June 1954 the purchase of a Church manse was **Jun** completed; funding for this had come in the form of a **1954** loan from the Baptist Union; the purchase price was £3600 plus £100 stamp duty and legal fees. The loan was made at 4% interest and it was hoped that it would only be required for a short time until the old Church land had been sold. This wish was fulfilled as the sale of the old Church land was soon completed for £4240. The author is unable to establish if this is the same piece of land that was on the market the year before for 10,000. If so, why the significant decrease in value?

Jun 1955 In June 1955 the singing of anthems led by the choir was discussed. It was felt much more appropriate if the choir were to be modelled on the "Haringey/Wembley" lines used at the Billy Graham Rallies. This was agreed. At the same meeting the Deacons notified the members that a search was being made for a more suitable manse, which needed to be more convenient to the Church and town. Later that year Victor Rowe was made a Life Deacon and the office of Elder made permanent for Victor Rowe and Gilbert Simmons.

By January 1956 negotiations were in progress to purchase a plot of land for the building of the new manse. It was also decided that the time had come to set up Kingfield as a separate Church. This was **Apr 1956** achieved on 10 April 1956 and ninety members formed the nucleus of the congregation. The property, at Kingfield, which was owned by Percy Street was also handed over.

One matter which provoked the members to write a letter to the Government was the introduction of Government Premium Bonds; these were believed by members to be a form of gambling. A reply was received which said that, in the Government's eye, this was not the case.

Towards the end of 1956 and early 1957 the Baptist Union agreed to make a loan of £4000 at 4.5% for a short period for the new manse and also to become its trustees. Building of the manse for £4018 was agreed at the lowest tender, with the aim of completion by November 1957.

In February 1957 the combined accounts for 1956 **Feb** showed an income of £3282 6s 5d and in September **1957** 1957 a "good neighbours" letter including an invitation to the film "Eastward to Asia" formed part of the Church's outreach programme.

Leslie Fraser's ministry ended during 1958, but the **1958** reason for his departure is not recorded in the Church minutes.

CHAPTER 7

THE PACE QUICKENS

Pastor: Philip Jones 1959 to 1965

At a Special Church Meeting held in April 1958 **Apr** Stanley Harrison was invited to act as the Church **1958** moderator following the departure of Leslie Fraser. There followed a search for a new full time Pastor. Following several names being brought to members' attention Philip Jones, from South Street Exeter, was invited to become pastor on 10 January 1959 (90% in favour). He agreed to start on 12 April 1959. One of the questions raised was the provision of a car. It was agreed to purchase his existing car and then purchase a new one when finance permitted.

Philip Jones introduced a number of changes shortly after his arrival. The Young People's Bible Class was merged to become part of the Adult Bible School, the Keswick Hymnal used as a trial for Sunday Morning communion services and combined bread and wine containers introduced.

The changes did not stop there - communion was introduced before the service on the first Sunday evening of the month, as this would allow the young people to take part in the Sunday "late night special"; giving to the missionary field was allocated on a fixed percentage of giving (2/3 Cynthia Goodall - teaching in the Far East, 1/3 Peter and Sunny Murray – in South America); and a poster was placed on Woking Station advertising the Church (November 1959).

Feb 1960 The seeds of a new outreach work commenced in February 1960 when authority to purchase amplifying, tape recording and radio equipment was given (£250 needed, £110 already promised). In the fullness of time this would become "Wondrous Story Radio Mission."

On 31 March 1960 it was decided to transfer the **Mar** Sunday School to the morning and adopt the Scripture **1960** Press Scheme. The "All Ages Sunday School" would commence at 09:45 and be followed by the normal worship service from 11:00 to 12:00. This was accepted. At the same time, it was agreed to shorten the length of the notices, by printing them on a sheet of paper for attendees.

"Late night Sunday specials" were not held during the summer months, evening communion was restored to its original time and carpeting for the aisles purchased. Also, there were complaints about the sounding of fire sirens during Church services. By July there is the first mention of the monthly Friday night prayer meeting (8pm to midnight) and operation "Water and Fire" where all organisations were required to have an evangelistic emphasis.

With the development of the Hermitage Woods Estate,

new opportunities opened up and eleven children started attending Percy Street (October 1960). Not only were there local opportunities, but also the Far Eastern Broadcasting Corporation (FEBC) asked if Wondrous Story Radio Mission could produce thirteen fifteen-minute gospel tapes for broadcast from Manila (capital of the Philippines). For Church members who could not physically attend Church services it was decided to relay the services over the telephone network.

Dec 1960 On 5 December 1960 a new set of Church rules was agreed by members; under these it became a requirement to set and publicise the date of the Annual General Meeting (the next being 6 March 1961). At the meeting in March it was reported that problems were being encountered at the "late night special" with the young people causing a nuisance in the toilets and not attending the meeting. The first serious attempt at producing a fifteen-minute programme for FEBC was played to members. At the same meeting the Church Secretary reported that the crèche had six or seven babies, Sunday School thirty three, Adult Bible Class twenty three, the Boys' Club now ran a football team, a Girls' Club had recently been set up for girls older than twelve, Junior Christian Endeavour had a membership of twelve eight to twelve year olds, Christian Endeavour had regular meetings (late night specials, local cafes), thirty to thirty five attended the women's meeting, the women's evening group had sixteen attendees, men's meeting sixteen attendees, radio recording committee met weekly (Manila and Liberia), and Sunday and Thursday services were being relayed to the Pines (a local home for the elderly). The requirement for a formal financial budget was also agreed.

At a Church Meeting on 24 July 1961 there was a **Jul** request to start a Life Boys group which would act as **1961** a feeder to the Boys Brigade. How to handle the possible post bag generated from tapes relayed in Manila and Liberia was discussed in October and help was sought together with prayer warriors.

At a Special Church Meeting held on 6 November Bob Boorman was elected as the Assistant Church Secretary and at the next meeting the sale of the pews was discussed. It was reported that the new lighting, wiring and boiler were all operating and that it was hoped to start exterior decoration shortly.

Jan 1962 On 29 January 1962 it was announced that there would be an Easter Bible School for children aged two to fourteen and the combined accounts for 1961 showed an income of £4156 14s 5d. Also notice was given that, after twenty-eight years in office as Church Secretary, Gilbert Simmons would be retiring and that the Sunday School had for the first time for many years one hundred attendees (fifty primary, fifty junior) with twenty to thirty children per week attending from the Hermitage Woods Estate. Reports from other organisations were also very positive e.g. the Boys' Football Team had only lost one match in two seasons and a successful young people's weekend had been held at Ventnor, Isle of Wight.

On 16 April 1962 it was announced that the target for **Apr** redecoration was £1000 and only £160 was **1962** outstanding, £120 to £140 was required for the purchase of the new Baptist Hymnal and a system of pastoral delegates was going to be set up. The delegates would help the Pastor with preliminary work and each member informed who their delegate was.

On 23 July 1962 it was announced that £300 was still **Jul** needed for the completion of the redecoration work at **1962** the Church flat and the manse and that the third Ventnor Youth Weekend would be held in October. Discussions took place concerning the setting up of a pilot scheme "Church Night" in the middle of the week (18:15 to 21:15). On this evening the majority of activities, normally held throughout the week would take place. A proposal was put forward concerning the use of either the "Fact & Faith" or Billy Graham films during three winter evening services.

On 22 October 1962 the Wondrous Story Radio **Oct** Mission was set up as a specific department of the **1962**

Church. The prayer meeting, Bible study and youth fellowship all now met on one weekday evening.

Mar At the Annual General Meeting held on 4 March 1963
1963 the combined accounts showed an income of £4791 4s 6d and Leslie Gloster thanked members for their excellent giving. Work with the children was expanding; the Sunday School had one hundred and nineteen children, the first Easter Bible School more than one hundred attendees and the Co-operative Society's hall was being used for children's Sunday worship (despite reports that it was dirty). The possibility of opening a new Sunday School on the Hermitage Woods Estate was discussed and shortly afterwards Hermitage Woods School was hired, despite the Headmistress being concerned about the school remaining in its new condition. The school would be used from 09:30 to 10:30 for children aged up to eleven; thirty-five to forty children are reported to have attended in June/July.

In March it was noted that Alan Sussex would be

responsible for organising an evangelistic mission run by the Inter Varsity Fellowship, the Girls Life Brigade had been formed and the first Sunday evening youth service would be held on 28 April 1963. Concern was also voiced about the Baptist Union sending a representative to attend a requiem service for the late Pope.

On 24 October the Missionary Council provision for Peter & Sunny Murray's financial arrangements was discussed; it was decided that insurance/pension cover would be set up for them and in January 1964 it was **Jan** agreed that the Church should purchase a 16mm cine **1964** projector for £300.

The age at which a person could become a Church member was discussed by members at two church meetings as two young teenagers had asked for membership. Concern was expressed about their attendance at Church meetings, where some subjects unsuitable for discussion before them may arise.

At the Annual General Meeting, held on 5 March **Mar** 1964, it was reported that the combined income was **1964**

£5431 6s 6d; overall the organisations were doing very well, and that Church membership was over two hundred. Problems with the caretaker at Hermitage Wood School were being experienced and it was suggested that it might be more practical to provide a bus to bring the children into Woking, rather than continue at the school.

On 30 April it was agreed that the Church would support Billy Graham's Earls Court rallies and that the Pastor's car would be replaced with an Austin A55. The car would be the Pastor's property, and he would be given a loan to purchase it and an allowance to meet its running costs. In July the question of whether to keep the gospel to ourselves or actively evangelise was discussed and amongst the many ideas put forward was the idea of having a strategic plan. At the same meeting it was decided to stop the "Late Night Sunday Special" because it had become impossible to conduct any evangelism with the people who attended! The subject of Eldership was raised, and it was pointed out that this subject was found in the

Bible!

On 29 October 1964 the Boys Brigade leaders **Oct** reported that a platoon would be formed. Fifty-one **1964** (including leaders) had attended the most recent Ventnor Youth Weekend. The subject of Church seating was raised; the chairs were narrow and uncomfortable and £500 was required to improve the seating, but only £150 had been received. Three courses of action were proposed:

- Spend the money to buy new chairs and add others when funding became available.
- Hold the money until the full amount had been raised, then purchase the chairs.
- Allocate the money to another use. (Note: at a Special Church meeting held on 28 January 1965 it was decided to go with this option).

At the October meeting the subject of Eldership was again raised, and it was agreed that the Pastor would go through the Bible teaching on the subject at the

Tuesday evening meetings. It was also agreed that attending Church prayer meetings should be everybody's priority.

Jul On 22 July 1965 it was agreed that home prayer
1965 meetings would take place on the fifth Tuesday of months containing five Tuesdays. At the same meeting the Pastor gave notice that his pastorate would terminate on 31 December 1965, with his final service on 2 January 1966. He had been invited to become the first full-time organising secretary for Far East Broadcasting Associates in the UK. Graham Swift had agreed to act as moderator. It was also announced that a proposal concerning Church Eldership would be made soon.

An extract from the Church magazine for August 1965 showing the Church leaders together with weekly activities is given in Appendix D, Figure 16. Figure 17 presents a collage of other weekly news/information sheets that were published between the years 1971 and 1988.

At a Special Church Meeting held on 28 October 1965 **Oct** the proposal concerning Eldership was brought to **1965** members' attention. Elders would "Rule and guide in matters affecting the spiritual wellbeing of the Church, maintain an evangelical emphasis in the pulpit ministry and assist the Pastor". Nine members were elected as Elders.

CHAPTER 8

NEW GROWTH, THE OUTPOURING OF THE HOLY SPIRIT, A "MOUNTAIN" AND A TIME OF TRANSITION

Pastor: Harold Owen 1967 to 1988

Jan On 27 January 1966 discussions concerning the
1966 selection of a new Pastor commenced. It was agreed
that he should:

- Be a conservative evangelical and Bible based.
- Be interested in the Wondrous Story Radio Mission and other missionary interests.

- Have a good character and love for pastoral work.
- Have a wife who would make an effective contribution and give the lead in the women's work.

The selection procedure was also discussed. The Baptist Union Area Superintendent would be contacted, and any interested ministers discussed, Church members would be invited to make suggestions and the Elders and Deacons would actively research the matter. The Elders and Deacons would be unanimous before bringing the name of a prospective Pastor to Church members.

On 21 April 1966 there was a discussion about the lack of real prayer within the Church and there was further discussion about home prayer meetings. The Top Gear young people's evangelistic campaign 15 to 22 October run by a group of Churches in Woking, was set a budget of £400 and it was noted that £300 had been received to date. Rev Arthur Rose would **Apr 1966** lead the venture which would include free coffee, taped and live Christian pop music and gospel presentations. The venue for the event was the top floor of H W Gloster's Wholesalers Grocers in Church Street. It was also announced that Frank Wilson would speak at the forthcoming Youth Weekend at Ventnor. At this time no names for a new Pastor were forthcoming.

Aug From 20th to 27th August the first Families Camp,
1966 organised by Frank and Mary Payne was held at Swanage, Dorset. For those who attended this and those held in the following years, there were many highlights and strong friendships formed. Highlights of the first camp were Rev Peter Thornton's talks on the Person of Jesus Christ, the childrens' before breakfast Bible stories on the cliffs overlooking Durleston Head, the roaring camp bonfire and of course the out-door camping! At a subsequent Camp a very young Terry Virgo from Seaford Baptist Church became the Padre – a name which was to reoccur

some years later in the life of the Church.

On the 27 October 1966 it was agreed that Bible study **Oct** groups along the lines used by Billy Graham would be **1966** started; Jack Goode would be responsible for these conversational style groups. Names for a replacement Pastor were still not forthcoming. The combined accounts for the year showed a total income of £7347 7s 3d, of which missionary giving was £1287 (an increase of £159 over previous year). Once again very good progress across a wide range of organisations was noted. All ages Sunday School took place every Sunday morning at 09:45 and there were forty-five children in the primary age group. Anthony's Sunday School had fifteen children, Friday Boys Club forty members (speakers had included Alec Bedser, the England Cricketer), and a trip around a telephone exchange and water company had taken place, Church services were being relayed to three people who could not attend and Wondrous Story Radio Mission had produced fifty-two fifteen minute programmes. (See Appendix D, Figure 18 for photo of the choir recording.)

Jan Finding a replacement pastor had not proved to be a
1967 quick process but on 5 and 31 January 1967 two
Special Church Meetings were held to consider the
possibility of inviting Harold Owen, Carey Street
Baptist Church, Reading to take on the responsibility.
The Elders had met with Harold Owen on 12
December to discuss the possibility of this. 94% of
attendees at the Special Church Meeting were in
favour of asking him to preach for a second time. At
the second meeting, where one hundred and seven
were present, ninety-eight voted for him to be asked to
become the next pastor (92%). This offer was
accepted, and Harold Owen commenced his
appointment in June 1967.

Mar At the Annual General Meeting held on 2 March 1967
1967 it was reported that the primary accommodation was
too small, there having been a 20% increase in
numbers in the Junior and Senior Bible classes. Ten
children attended Anthony's Sunday School, Girls

Life Brigade had been given a new look[5], Boys Club had thirty attendees each week, Young people had new leaders (Pat & Jenny Prosser) and there was a new-look coffee bar where the emphasis was on evangelism, Bible study and discussion. The interregnum had not been a period of stagnation or recession. With regard to missionary work Margaret Wickens had joined the Baptist Federation in Paris and Janet Robinson had started a course at Moorlands Bible College. These were in addition to those currently working overseas (Peter and Sunny Murray and Cynthia Goodall).

On 20 April the need for a rebuilding scheme was discussed. Geoff Perkins outlined a proposal for an extension, general improvements and how this fitted in with the Woking Town Centre Scheme. There had

Apr 1967

---

[5] From the record just what this involved is unclear, but it coincides reasonably with the amalgamation of three similar bodies in 1964 – the Girls' Brigade of Ireland, the Girls' Guildry of Scotland and the Girls' Life Brigade of England

been the possibility of re-developing the Church on a new central site, with costs coming from the sale of the existing premises. However, this had ceased to be viable as the Government had put an embargo on the development of new offices; therefore, the potential for the sale of the existing premises had declined. It was concluded that it was right to develop the existing premises which had virtually remained unaltered for forty years. A proper kitchen, toilet, meeting room, replacement hut, and possibly a purpose-built studio for Wondrous Story Radio Mission was suggested. It was hoped that the upper floor of two of the cottages next to the Church could be modernised for the caretaker. An application for the kitchen modifications had been submitted to the planning department of Woking Borough Council. The cost for the kitchen, excluding fittings was estimated to be around £1000. It was felt that the Council were unlikely to oppose the replacement of the hut with a permanent structure.

During the summer of 1967 there was a lot of discussion concerning the Boys Brigade and a new

Captain was required to take through some proposed changes. Planning permission for the kitchen had been received, but a Special Church Meeting was required to agree the expenditure. A week of prayer was announced, and members were asked to fill centre seats for communion, to avoid unnecessary noise at Sunday services.

At a Special Church Meeting on 26 October 1967 **Oct** financial approval for the new kitchen was given **1967** (£1200 - £500 from deposit account, £300 from current account, £400 from gift days). It was also announced that a Doctrinal Basis of Belief was being drawn up and sermons would go through these statements in turn. The money held over from the chairs project was donated to a project in the Seychelles. A little surprisingly, it is recorded in January 1968 that one hundred chairs had been ordered for the hall. A matter of concern was with the organisation of the Woking Christian Council - a Roman Catholic Father had been elected to the Executive Committee. After consideration it was decided to withdraw from the Council. The total membership of the Church had now reached two hundred and twenty-one.

Mar 1968 At the Annual General Meeting held on 7 March 1968, it was reported that in future all those who held responsibilities within the Church would be required to be baptised Church members. The combined accounts for the year showed an income of £9345 19s 0d. Harold Owen preached on Sundays, not to mention Tuesdays, on the need for personal revival, holiness and the need for a deep work of the Holy Spirit. The Church hall had been bursting at the seams on Tuesday evenings. Whilst the young people's Coffee Bar had been reasonably successful in that dozens of people had heard the gospel and the coffee had achieved quite a reputation, the end results were less than hoped for.

Apr 1968 On 25 April 1968 it was reported that the main kitchen structure had been completed, missionary giving had been allocated as follows: 10% bursary, 30% Baptist

Missionary Society, 20% Overseas Missionary Fellowship, 20% WEC (now Worldwide Evangelisation for Christ) and 20% Baptist Homework Fund. The dual role of Deacons and Elders was to be dropped, leaving five Deacons. Disquiet with the Baptist Union, who wanted more involvement with the Ecumenical Movement, was expressed; should the Church resign its membership?

On 25 July 1968 the future of Anthony's was discussed. Was there still a real need? **Jul 1968**

On 31 October 1968 it was agreed that the Doctrinal Basis for Faith would be incorporated into Church membership application forms. The final cost of the kitchen, including fittings, had risen to £1900. Members recorded three points:

- Disappointment about the costs
- Sympathy re the costs
- The pleasure of the ladies who could use the new facilities

The Church membership now totalled between two hundred and thirty and two hundred and forty. Members were assigned for matters relating to illness and need, to one of the Oversight. God was really blessing the Young People especially in the evangelistic work in the Coffee Bar. This was not an emotional upsurge, lives were being changed and there was a deep work of the Holy Spirit which was beginning to infect the rest of the Church. The events surrounding this outpouring of the Holy Spirit are recounted here by Bryan Cross.

Sep "Shortly before I became a Church member Harold
1968 Owen had been away to a University Students' gathering and God had met many of the students and filled them with the Holy Spirit, something that was new to many of us. At the following Tuesday night prayer meeting the Pastor shared what had happened. Afterwards there was a feeling among a few of the young men that they would like to hear more.

"Peter Smith arranged with the Pastor for the young

men to meet with him three days later on the Friday evening in, what was called at that time, the Upper Room. The Pastor invited two Church members, David Kirkland and David Parson, to come with him as they both had similar experiences of the Holy Spirit.

"From memory because the meeting was arranged at very short notice, only about five or six young men were able to attend. The Pastor shared with us about the Holy Spirit and referred to various passages in the scriptures about His working and the manifestations of the Spirit. He then asked us, individually, to read through Psalm 51 and to ask God to cleanse us from our sin and ensure that we were right before Him. We were then encouraged to ask God to fill us. Each had to seek God individually, but the Pastor was there to help.

"During that evening and over the next few days God met us in a very special way. The following evening was the Young People's Coffee Bar and I believe that was the first night that someone became a Christian. Following these events, the Holy Spirit transformed the work amongst other Christian young people who were part of the Coffee Bar and many became Christians in a relatively short space of time, then it began to spill over into other areas of the Church.

"Whilst this new and exciting work was gladly accepted by many of the members, others were much more cautious, and others felt compelled to leave the Church and worship elsewhere."

Jan 1969 On 31 January 1969 it was reported that plans to knock down the two cottages and hut had not been brought to the attention of members as it was uncertain that in its current form it would gain Woking Borough Council approval. The plan was to replace the buildings with a larger structure including a flat on the top floor for the caretaker. There would also be a forecourt with service access for builders etc.

During April to September 1969 a visitation scheme was introduced with Bryan Cross as co-ordinator.

Letters were sent to homes in the area, followed by visits from members in pairs. Each pair was allocated one or two roads.

At the Annual General Meeting, Leslie Gloster retired **Mar** after twenty years as Treasurer and was succeeded by **1969** Geoff Owers. The combined accounts for the Church showed an income of £11,681 14s 4d. The number of children from Hermitage Woods had decreased. In contrast, the young people's work had grown considerably from twenty-five to seventy-five. The Church Secretary records that "most noticeable amongst young people and the Coffee Bar was 'They had been troubled, burdened and felt completely inadequate to work for God..... until it pleased God that He didn't want them to work for Him but He longed to work through them... eagerness and joy in young people' ". During the year there had been an emphasis on the third person of the Trinity, the Holy Spirit. Thirty-seven new members had joined the Church.

Apr
1969 On 24 April 1969 it was reported that Woking Borough Council were of the view that in the proposed development the Church were trying to include too much on the site.

By July 1969 it was proposed to re-style the inside of the Church to increase its overall seating capacity. It was estimated that the work would cost around £200 and involve moving the existing pulpit railing, having a portable pulpit, new carpet, backdrop and two spotlights. Additionally, new pews were being considered for the main body of the Church at £5 to £9 per seat run. Also, it was proposed that the school hall would be decorated during August and the young people asked not to play ball games once it had been decorated. David Kirkland reported that planning permission in principle had been obtained for the demolition of the hut and cottages, building of a new hall, toilets and a caretaker's flat. Access would be from Church Street. It was agreed that the work would be funded by direct giving.

During 1969 problems with the Baptist Union continued and questions were asked by members concerning who the leaders and Church could relate to if we withdrew. The Pastor was of the view that we could relate to other Churches within the Baptist Church movement who were also concerned about the need for revival.

On 30 October 1969 it was announced that the local **Oct** planning committee had approved the overall site **1969** development, but a final decision was awaited from the North West Surrey Planning Committee. Permission to proceed with building a new hall and caretaker's flat on the land of 11 and 13 Percy Street was received.

At the Annual General Meeting held on 5 March **Mar** 1970, Josh Nunn reported that there were one hundred **1970** and sixty-four under fifteen's in regular attendance with 85% on any one Sunday with a high proportion from non-Church homes. At Anthony's all the children in the vicinity (seventeen) attended the

Sunday School. Other activities were the first full year of Cabin Boys (thirteen), Young Wives led by Olive Davis (twenty-five) and Boys Club (five to six). The young people had distributed invitations to the Coffee Bar in Woking which was open on Saturday evenings, five hundred and two homes had been identified for visitation evangelism (forty-five empty or demolished, no contact with fifty-five, four hundred and two responses, one hundred and sixteen second visit). The Church Secretary reported that during the autumn and winter of 1968/9 the Church had experienced much blessing from God but now there was something of a lull.

Apr 1970 On 30 April 1970 the use of the Church-owned shops was discussed. Existing tenants had terminated their stay and there was no intention to sub-let. It was suggested that the windows could be used for display purposes. Other alternatives were invited. With regard to the new building work, access to the site was discussed; it was estimated that the project would cost

£30,000 but how was this to be raised?

At a Special Church Meeting held on 14 May 1970, **May** the site development and new Church seating were **1970** discussed (5 quotations for the pews from £2000 to £7000 – seventy-two members voted for the expensive pews with only nine against). By October an architect had been briefed to design a large hall, caretaker's flat, toilet block, entrance hall, connection to the existing building and Wondrous Story Radio Mission booth with access to the building being from Church Street. The overall cost of the work was estimated to be £42,000, but was there a cheaper way?

At the Annual General Meeting, held on 25 March **Mar** 1971 it was reported that Sunday School attendance **1971** had increased by 30% during the year (friends and Brigades), there were eighty three primary and seventy five beginners on a Sunday, the Crèche had twenty four, the Boys Brigade was also thriving, Boys Club now under the leadership of Michael Chambers had fifteen boys, Wondrous Story Radio Mission had celebrated its 10th anniversary, the Young People's Coffee Bar was going really well and on 7 November eighteen soldiers from Pirbright Army Camp had come into the Coffee Bar, heard the gospel and returned to the Church on the following Sunday evening. The Church Secretary reported that most of the missionaries were on furlough and Rita Chan had joined Life for the World.

Last year it had been reported that there had been a lull in spiritual progress, but things had changed during the year, the Pastor had been challenged by God and there had been a new liberty in praise and prayer. For example, the mid-week prayer meeting which used to end at 21.00 had been extended by half an hour. The active membership of the Church was now two hundred and fifty (twenty people had been baptised and eleven new members added during the year). With regard to the building plans, £500 had been offered to the Council for the access strip, three builders had been approached and they had indicated that the work would cost around £25,000 and take six months to complete.

On 15 May 1971 Malcolm Simpson, the Church **May** Secretary, informed members that the Church had sent **1971** a letter to the Baptist Union concerning the "Deity of Christ" controversy. A response was received on 18 May and at the quarterly Church meeting held on 29 July 1971, the issue was discussed, and it was decided **Jul** to wait until the Baptist Union Council had met in **1971** November. About the development, the building sub-committee had agreed that the tender from Reema was their preferred option and that drawings had been placed with Woking Borough Council. There was still a question concerning the access strip of land.

On 28 October 1971 it was announced that the go- **Oct** ahead for the development was expected by the end of **1971** the year. Questions were asked about what would happen to the young people's work during the rebuilding.

In December 1971 the Church Secretary wrote to all **Dec** members concerning the Baptist Union issue; this was **1971** in preparation for a Church Meeting arranged for 6

Jan January 1972. At this meeting it was agreed by one

1972 hundred and seven to twenty-eight to withdraw from Baptist Union and shortly afterwards it was proposed to form an Association of Evangelical Baptist Churches.

On 27 January 1972 it was reported that progress with the development work was not going as swiftly as expected. Woking Borough Council was trying to sell the corner car park site by the traffic lights on Victoria Way and Church Street West - where Toys R Us eventually stood for many years and this inevitably complicated the arrangements for the Church development. The Council had approached the Church to see if it was interested in becoming a member of a co-operative development with a third party. This option was refused on principle. Alternatively, the whole site including the Church property, could be sold and an alternative site for the Church found near the town centre. Additionally, Woking Borough Council had a developer interested in developing properties facing into Church Street. As a result of this it was agreed that the proposed Church development was back to square one.

At the Annual General Meeting held on 23 March **Mar** 1972, it was reported that there were swelling numbers **1972** at evening services, there had been thirty-nine new members added and forty-three people had been baptised during the year. The active membership was now two hundred and seventy. Numbers at Anthony's Sunday School were beginning to fall, eighty boys now attended Boys' Brigade on a Wednesday evening and the young people were in the process of renovating one of the shops as a centre for their operations. General expenses for the year were £7642.

On 5 May 1972 the way forward with the building **May** plan was again discussed; two options were **1972** considered:

- Proceed with the original plan.
- Sell the complete site and build a new one somewhere else. Approaches had been made

from outside companies to buy the existing
premises ranging from £100,000 to £348,000.

Members were asked to consider what the Lord
wanted us to do. On balance it was proposed to go
with the second option. There was no desire for capital
gain, although staying could mean that people would
see us as a "down-town" Church; if we stayed, we
would be committed to spending £30,000 - if we
moved a simple but adequate Church could be built.
Could Woking Borough Council be asked if there was
a one-acre site within ¾ mile of the town centre where
a new building could be constructed? Should we
employ professional advice? It was decided to go with
the second option with no delay as the financial offer
may not be maintained if delays were introduced.

Oct On 26 October 1972 it was reported that following an
1972 advertisement in the London Gazette one hundred and
fifty-six parties expressed an interest in developing the
Percy Street site. It was also decided to stop the long-
standing practice, initiated by Gilbert Simmons, of

supplying sweets to children after the morning service!

On 23 November 1972 it was reported that **Nov** negotiations were nearing completion through Mann **1972** and Co. with Brierfield Properties for the property development. Twenty-eight tenders had been received (from £290,000 to £401,000 for the freehold). The Trustees were soon to sign the documents. Arrangements had been made with Mann and Co. to purchase the freehold of 5 Oaks Road, 55 to 59 Goldsworth Road and 1 Church Street. Negotiations were also in progress concerning the purchase of 3 Church Street. The new property would be about twice the size of the Percy Street site. A resolution to go ahead was passed with only one exception (eighty-two present).

By 25 January 1973 good progress had been made **Jan** with the development plans. Mann and Co. had **1973** submitted plans to the Council for two showrooms and offices, and for a change of use for the Percy Street site. No 1 Church Street had been purchased for £9750, the Goldsworth Road/Oaks Road property for £35,000 and there were negotiations in place for the purchase of No 3 Church Street at a price of £15,000. Reema had provided a sketch of how the new building might look.

Mar At the Annual General Meeting on 29 March 1973, it
1973 was announced that a decision on the selection of the architect was awaited and that the bank was prepared to make the necessary loans. There was £7,000 in the building fund, investment and fees amounted to £45,000 and this meant an overdraft of £38,000 (at 11%). Away from development matters it was recorded that membership was now up to two hundred and seventy-five and that prayer meetings on two occasions had not finished until 10.30.

May On the 3 May 1973 it was announced that an architect
1973 had been appointed to draw up plans for the new Church. However, the initial plans submitted by Reema were unsuitable and outline planning

permission for the new Church had not been approved. The Church caretaker was now living at 1 Church Street whilst alterations to 5 Oaks Road were being made. The first signs of trouble to come started to appear in that the loans required for the purchase of the houses were subject to a rising interest rate!

In July 1973 Michael Maughan met with the Pastor to **Jul** explore the possibility of him becoming more closely **1973** associated with the Church; after meeting with the other leaders a time of special prayer was held on 27 September. The outcome of which, followed by a Special Church Meeting was that Michael Maughan was invited to become a full time Elder assisting the Pastor. Michael took up his new position in November 1973.

On 2 August 1973 it was reported that the Church now **Aug** owned all of the required properties (1, 3 Church **1973** Street, 55 to 57 and 59 Goldsworth Road and 5 Oaks Road which was occupied by the caretaker.) Approval had been given for the development of the site. The architect had done his preliminary work and the Church now had an outstanding loan of £60,000, with outgoings servicing the loan and the architect's fees of £800 to £900. Unfortunately, an economic crisis then hit the UK with consequential rising interest rates on loans and the creation of a stagnant property market. Almost overnight, all possible buyers for the Church property withdrew. The Church found itself with a large financial debt and the leadership were faced with

Jan a serious problem. By January 1975 it was stated in
1975 the Church's weekly news sheet (Announcer) that the debt had risen to £66,833, "representing £220 per member or two hundred and fifty colour TV sets or £500 a week for the next three years". It continued "in fact, we have seen a miracle to date".

Mar The financial situation became worse over the coming
1975 months, coming to a head one Sunday in March 1975. Instead of a normal Sunday sermon, the Pastor outlined the Church's financial situation. The Church had a massive bridging loan which was attracting monthly bank charges. At that date the debt stood at

£80,000. Whilst members had generously contributed money to resolve the shortfall the capital was not being reduced, in fact it was still growing. Members were asked to think and pray concerning how to reduce the debt. Harold Owen announced that here would be a "giving morning" in seven days' time.

After communion on the following Sunday, members each gave as they felt able. By lunchtime £42,000 had been given or promised. There were no specific large gifts, and nothing was contributed from the other Church funds; rather, everybody gave something; some sold their cars, others jewellery, cameras, others gave cash and some IOUs. Overall this worked out as an average of £120 per member. This was an amazing Sunday and never to be forgotten by those who attended - it became known as "Mountain Sunday".

Whilst all were amazed, some were a little disappointed as they had believed that God would provide the full amount. God had other plans. He had taught members a lesson on giving and this resulted in the unlocking of people's hearts and money over the coming months.

The need for larger, more suitable premises remained but the way forward was unclear. The Church owned both the Percy Street building and site and property in Goldsworth Road. The Church leadership were of the view that God would have to once again intervene.

This God did, and only months later a property developer offered to design and build free of charge a purpose-built Church on the land owned by the Church in Goldsworth / Oaks Roads in exchange for the property and land in Percy Street. This offer was gladly accepted, and events started to happen very quickly.

All of the required planning permissions were obtained and it was agreed that the first stage of the work would be to demolish the building in Percy Street. The last service was held in Percy Street on the **Dec** 31 December 1976. The Church was faced with the **1976** prospect of having nowhere to meet whilst the building work took place.

A temporary home for the congregation was offered by two local Churches. Sunday afternoon services were held, with the kind permission of Rev Bishop, at Trinity Methodist Church in Brewery Road and other activities at St Mary of Bethany Church in York Road.

The new Church premises, holding three hundred and fifty in the Chapel, one hundred in the Hall plus a further one hundred and fifty in a coffee area were opened on 8 October 1977 with Nellie Hicks, one of **Oct** the longest serving members, formally handing over **1977** the keys of the new building to the Pastor. The building was named "The Coign", which is an old English word meaning cornerstone or vantage point. The name was chosen for three main reasons:

- In the New Testament Jesus is referred to as the cornerstone and foundation of the Church
- The building itself was in a strategic position being at one of the main entrances to Woking Town Centre

- To take people's attention away from the generally accepted view that the building was the Church. The New Testament refers to the Church as the members at a specific location

A brief service of dedication followed and in excess of one thousand cups of tea were served to visitors during the day. The opening day closed with a service of praise.

In the Church Secretary's report for 1976 it is recorded that "after nine years of effort, worry and frustration suddenly the Lord moved, and it was all so simple. The last residue of the debt was paid. The money, Woking Borough Council planning, the actual building, clearing of the old building, where to go whilst we were without a building, what to do without a vestry…. there are no problems in Heaven, only plans. Church meetings became enjoyable, fifty-two new members had joined the Church and forty-four were baptised". In the previous year (1975) the Church had an overdraft of £67,000, but by 1 January

1976 this had reduced to £19,000. By the time the new building was opened the debt had been eliminated.

Tuesday "Praise nights", as they had become by 1977, **1977** were often very exciting and God was so clearly present. During one of these in June the following prophecy was given "My children I am teaching you that healing, to me, is of the whole man and so much of the needs of men and women today, even their physical sicknesses, are the outcome of tortured minds, of unhappy hearts, of bitter spirits and broken relationships ……. I will make this people a people of healing and into this company I desire to bring those who are sick, not just in body but in mind and spirit and in heart……. I will heal ……… for if I am to be the Healer amongst you, you must be a healed people……."

During 1977 a proposal was made by John Watkins, a Trustee, to modify the structure by which the Pastor was provided with accommodation. For many years the Church had owned or rented a house for the Pastor and his family. Amongst other reasons it was recognised that continuation of this practice could lead to a situation where on retirement the Pastor would have no accommodation to go to. Overall it was felt that, as a good employer, the Church had a duty of care for the long-term future of the Pastor. Following discussions with the Charity Commission and Church members it was agreed to sell the manse and provide an interest free loan to the Pastor so that he could purchase his own house.

Jan 1978 In January 1978 it was announced that Howard Dodge would commence full-time employment with the Church; his responsibilities would include co-ordinating the new house-group system.

Mar 1978 At the Annual General Meeting, held on 30 March 1978, the Church Secretary reported that thirty-six new members had joined the Church in the previous twelve months and there had been fifty-one baptisms. Also, there had been an increase in the number of links with other Churches outside the immediate locality, including Holland, Belgium, Malaysia, Wales, Sheffield, Chesterfield and Reading. There had been a remarkable increase in giving since 1973 (30% increase in weekly offerings – giving a new average weekly offering of £606). A quarter of the giving had been received as a result of members using the Government Covenant Tax Refund scheme. The building fund had been finally closed, but there were plans to build an out-building behind the Coign (authority to build a games room/garage behind the Coign at an estimated £6500 was subsequently granted on 2 August 1978).

A major change in Church Government was brought before members on 25 May 1978. It was proposed and agreed that the Church would become a Church run by an Eldership, rather than the more democratic style adopted to date. **May 1978**

Over the winter of 1978/9 it was recognised that affordable housing in the Woking area was becoming difficult for people to obtain. This was particularly the **1979**

137

case for young married couples, singles and those with limited or no income. To help those in need, exploratory discussions took place to determine whether a Church housing association could be formed. On investigation it was established that this was not possible but that it may be feasible to set up a charitable trust.

Mar 1979 At the Annual General Meeting held on 22 March 1979 the Church Secretary reported that during the previous twelve months thirty-six people had been welcomed into Church membership and forty had been baptised. It was noted that The Coign building would soon not be big enough to host Sunday praise nights with other Churches. It was also agreed that those who attended House Groups in the Kingfield area could move to Kingfield Church (New Life).

Jan 1980 By early January 1980 the shortage of sufficient space on Sundays and mid-week was becoming a major issue. In particular there was a shortage of counselling rooms on a Sunday evening, the lounge was too small for the Central house-group, with its thirty-five members, to meet mid-week and there was a need for a seminar room for meeting with other Church leaders. Consequently, the architect who designed the Coign had been approached and he proposed either building in front of the existing premises over the garden area or building on stilts in the car park. The extension plans were further considered at the Annual General Meeting held on 27 March 1980. An extension costing **Mar** an estimated £40,000 was proposed, but no final **1980** decision concerning the way forward was taken. At the same meeting it was agreed to sell the Church building and land at Anthony's.

At the Special Church Meeting which was also held on 27 March 1980, it was proposed to set up a charitable trust (The Coign Trust) "to enable assistance to be given to members in the fellowship who had housing or financial needs".

Problems concerning the need for additional space were once again drawn to members' attention in

September 1980. It was said that overall there was no vision for extending the building for congregational purposes, although it was recognised that with continued growth there may come a time when consideration should be given to splitting into more than one congregation for Sunday worship, but retaining the central facility for administration and ministry. However, it was recognised that whatever happened in the future concerning congregations, a new Church lounge was still required. Consequently, members were asked for commitment to build a new lounge at a cost of £40,000, half of which was already available. It was proposed that the work should start in the spring of 1981 with completion by the end of the summer. All those at the meeting gave their support to this building plan.

Mar On 19 March 1981 it was reported that the Church had
1981 a membership of three hundred and seventy-four and an average attendance of two hundred and eighty on a Sunday, sixty-three people had been baptised in the previous twelve months, forty-six new members added

and there were twenty-two House Groups which met during the week. There were one hundred and sixty children in the Church.

Offerings had increased by 25% and this was the first time that a weekly average of over £1000 had been given (£1189 per week). It was noted that ten years previously the £100 barrier had been reached. At the start of the year the funds had a balance of £24,000 and the year ended with £37,000. A gift day was announced for 5 April 1981, to help pay for the building work which had risen to £50,000; the target for the gift day was set at £10,000.

At the same meeting it was announced that, after seven and a half years of ministry, the resignation of Michael Maughan, as assistant Pastor, was received with sadness. It is interesting to note that the possibility of Church membership totalling two thousand members was raised!

In September 1981 it was announced that with the **Sep** Church's changing needs, Wondrous Story Radio **1981** outreach would cease at the end of the year. Over the years the Christian message had been faithfully proclaimed around the world by the Wondrous Story team. This included to Monrovia & Liberia (ELWA), Manila & Philippines (FEBC), Puerto Rico (WIVV), Seychelles (FEBA), Cyprus and Northern Ireland (British Forces Radio). At the meeting thanks was given to all involved and especially to Alice Potter.

At the same time as this work was closing there was a significant increase in the tape ministry, with copies of Sunday services being sent around the world.

Harold Owen explained that Terry Virgo was trying to bring together a number of Churches in the south of England under the name of "Coastlands" and that the relationship between him and the Church leadership was continuing to develop. It was proposed that this relationship should be explored further, and after discussion, it was decided to build a "no rigid" relationship with him.

Beyond Woking, help was being given to Churches in

Durham and Putney, Holland, Switzerland, and Austria.

The Christmas offering for the Eastern European Church was £4556. The Murray family were now back in the UK working for WEC in Leeds.

At the end of 1981 David Dennington became a full-time member of The Coign staff and on 1 April 1982, John Forrest joined as the Administrator. **1981**

At the Annual General Meeting in March 1982, at which there were two hundred present, reports were received regarding the work in the countries/towns mentioned above together with Crawley and Egham. Harold Owen had now officially joined the Coastlands Team and Terry Virgo had agreed to visit the Coign occasionally. It was announced that the first Sunday morning congregation (Horsell) would start meeting on 18 April 1982 at Sythwood School and the Sunday evening meeting at the Coign would take the form of a celebration. The Secretary reported that forty-five new members had been added to the Church during the **Mar 1982**

143

year and thirty-four people baptised. Twenty-four mid-week House Groups met regularly and building work consisting of a new meeting room, enlarged study and an office had been completed. The Treasurer reported that in 1965 offerings had been £60 per week (£3000 per year) compared with the recent year when an average of £1344 per week had been received.

Mar 1983 At the Annual General Meeting held in March 1983 it was announced that it was the Elders' intention to start a second congregation to be established for people living in the Knaphill area, in September 1983. Whilst at this time only one (and soon to be two) of the congregations met separately on a Sunday morning, all the Church membership had been divided into five congregations with each being led by a senior leader. The number of new members had almost trebled during the year with a record of one hundred and twenty-six people added to membership and ninety-one baptisms.

At the Annual General Meeting held in March 1984, **Mar** at which two hundred and fifty members were present, **1984** the Church Secretary reported that the year had been a year of consolidation at Sythwood congregation, a second had begun in Knaphill and congregations for those who lived in Byfleet and Runnymede would commence between April and June.

Involvement with churches overseas continued in Austria, and in Basle and Lausanne both in Switzerland. In Durham attendance had now grown to one hundred and fifty in the morning and two hundred and fifty in the evening, meaning that the Church was now able to stand on its own and would in future relate to the Bradford Church.

During the year visits had been received from Terry Virgo, Alan Vincent, Henry Tyler, Ray Booth, Ray Lowe, Arthur Wallis and John Babu.

The Treasurer reported that the Church was currently known jointly as The Coign Fellowship and Woking Baptist Church but that it was intended to amend the

Church deeds to call the Church just The Coign Fellowship. Offerings over the year had exceeded £100,000 and average weekly offerings had reached £1982. At the meeting, members discussed the possibility of building a new kitchen and toilet extension.

Mar At the Annual General Meeting held in March 1985 it **1985** was reported that Church membership had reached five hundred and fifty, there were thirty-five House Groups with four Congregations meeting on a Sunday Morning (Horsell, Knaphill and at the Coign a mixture of Runnymede, Westfield and Byfleet. The fourth was a small group at Farncombe). Ninety-two people had been baptised and eighty-five new members added to the Church membership.

John Babu had visited the Church from India, a course called "One thing is needful" had been run for women and work on the extension to the kitchen was in progress. Ray and Jean Booth had joined the Church from Sheffield in January 1985 with Ray joining the staff shortly after.

At the Annual General Meeting held in 25 March **Mar** 1986 it was reported that during the year forty-nine **1986** people had been baptised and seventy-seven new members added. Sunday morning congregations had consolidated with Runnymede now meeting and South Woking due to start shortly. For much of the year House Groups had met, but during January 1986 new pastoral groups had been formed together with "Works of Service" and "Iron" groups – this was the biggest change to the internal system since the introduction of House Groups ten years before.

Ray and Jean Booth had now completed their first year at the Church. The treasurer reported that total offerings for the year had risen to £163,943 (with an average of £2876 per week). There were seven full time members of staff.

During the 1980's an amazing work of God occurred amongst the Travellers. It commenced when Henry and Esther Cooper were parked at Lakeview whilst waiting for a more permanent site to be made available at Worplesdon. Esther became ill and sought medical help from Dr James Mellor. During her illness a number of Church members prayed for her and visited her in her caravan. Unfortunately, Esther did not recover, and her funeral service was held at the Church. This was a unique ceremony with many relatives and visitors in attendance together with a lorry full of flowers.

Good links with the Travellers were developed and David Dennington, encouraged by Ray Booth, asked Mike and Janet Phipps to lead a Travellers' House Group at their main site at Leatherhead. Other Church members including Jim and Chris Cousins, John and Sybil Ogden and Eileen Greenwood helped with the work. It is reported that thirty-five adults and ten to twelve children attended these meetings in a caravan.

A number of baptisms took place both at the Church in Woking and in the River Mole near Leatherhead and some significant healings took place, including an instant healing of a tumour behind Henry Cooper's daughter's eye. The healing was authenticated by medical staff at Redhill Hospital. On some Sunday evenings many of the adult Travellers along with their children would attend the Church service in Woking.

On 1st January 1987 Sean Larkin from Stanmore **Jan** joined the Ministry Team as a full time Elder. Around **1987** the same time David Brown also joined the team.

At the Annual General Meeting held in April 1987, **Apr** when three hundred were present it was announced **1987** that during the year there had been sixty baptisms and seventy-three new members added.

There were a number of changes which had been made or were soon to be made to the administration of the Church. Brian Checksfield had become a fulltime Elder/ Administrator and it was proposed that Eddie Bower, Ray Smith and Alan Sussex would become Elders with special responsibility for their congregations. Andrew Ryland had become the Knaphill Congregation Elder together with responsibility for evangelism. David Brown had become an Elder with the Horsell congregation and Sean Larkin an Elder with the Goldsworth congregation together with responsibility for healing ministry. Mark-Landreth Smith was now responsible for the young people's work.

Chas Davis reported that discussions with Sainsbury's had commenced concerning the possible development at the rear of the Coign site and that outline plans had already been drawn up.

The "Instow Project" to provide affordable accommodation was discussed; it was planned to purchase three flats in Cliff and Kath Davis's house, "Instow", Castle Road, and develop them into a number of units where the disadvantaged could have accommodation. (The plan could not subsequently be realised due to objections to the scheme received from neighbours as minuted in April 1989).

The Treasurer was pleased to report that there were now ten full-time members of staff and that the

Church was still financially sound. The average offering had risen to £3205 per week. At the start of 1987 Harold Owen had challenged everybody about finance and, as a result, the average offering in the first eight weeks of the year had risen to £4069 and had broken the £6000 barrier for the first time in March.

At the Annual General Meeting held in April 1988 it **Apr** was announced that the full-time Elders would be **1988** called the "Ministry team" and that they would be responsible for making executive decisions. Five congregations were now meeting (including Goldsworth Park led by Sean Larkin). In October the Chertsey Community Church under the leadership of David Dennington had been planted out.

Forty-eight people had been baptised and sixty had become members. Forty-one transfers from other Churches had taken place. One hundred and thirty-six had left the fellowship (seventy-two to Chertsey, forty-three moved away, fifteen resigned, three removed and three died). Overall the membership on 1 January 1988 was six hundred and thirty-one.

Average weekly offerings had risen to £4124 per week and total giving was £¼ million; 75% of the offerings had been used to pay the staff and £50,000 had been given away to thirty-six different people or organisations. Weekly offerings had dropped by £600 per week when the members involved with the Chertsey Community Church had left.

A new outreach ministry had recently commenced; the Christian Contact telephone helpline, and fourteen calls had been received within its first two weeks; seven calls had been trivial, four wanted to meet Coign people and one had attended a Sunday service.

Oct On the first Sunday in October 1988 Harold Owen
1988 officially retired as Pastor and handed over the leadership to Ray Booth. Towards the end of the year, it was decided to stop holding the Sunday morning meetings in separate congregations and return to a single central meeting. This new arrangement

commenced in January 1989. **1989**

Unfortunately, after only a brief period as leader of the Church, Ray Booth stepped down from his role. There followed an unsettled period for the Church as it was seeking to determine the best way forward.

To help resolve the leadership impasse Terry Virgo facilitated a meeting on 7 March 1989 which included **Mar** the full-time staff, Ben Davies and Malcolm Kayes, **1989** both from the Bracknell Family Church known as the Kerith Community Church. At that meeting Ray Booth, Sean Larkin and David Brown made it clear that they were unhappy with the revised internal arrangements for running the Church and as such did not see themselves as part of the future leadership.

Two days later, on 9 March 1989, a significant Quarterly Church Meeting was convened, and two hundred and seventy-five Church members were present. Ben Davies and Malcolm Kayes were also invited to attend. It commenced with discussions on the need for additional Church buildings and a "Think

Tank" was announced to consider all options including extending the current buildings and the purchase of new premises. The Church's links with New Frontiers International (NFI), the new name for Coastlands, was another significant agenda item. It was agreed that:

- The Coign should remain committed to NFI and receive apostolic cover from Terry Virgo and Ben Davies
- Malcolm Kayes would become more closely involved with The Coign until the future direction of the Church became clear. He would remain a member of the full-time staff at Bracknell
- All the Elders would lay down their responsibilities and see what emerged

Howard Dodge then opened the meeting for discussion. Sean Larkin and David Brown were not in agreement with the link to NFI. Ray Booth explained his confusion and difficulty over recent months concerning the Ministry Team and that he felt unable to lead the Church.

At that meeting on 9th March a significant prophecy was given "I am in the process of shaking my Church and I am in the process of shaking you and every security that you rely on in the face of man. Some of you have come tonight expecting Ben [Davies] to appoint a new leader of the Church and I say to you he has done that. My Son is your leader ….. I will build my security back ……".

On 14 March 1989 a note to all leaders was circulated **Mar** outlining the current leadership situation. Apart from **1989** summarising the events of 9 March 1989 it was announced that Howard Dodge would take responsibility for the overall leading with Brian Checksfield remaining as the Administrator. A meeting had been held on 13 March with Sean Larkin and David Brown where their positions were discussed and it was agreed that they would cease to be part of the leadership.

Apr At the Annual General Meeting held on 6 April 1989
1989 the leadership problems were discussed again. It was also announced that forty-five people had been baptised and forty-five had become Church members (nineteen of whom had recently become Christians). The Treasurer reported that, for the first time in twenty years, offerings and gifts had dropped from the previous year (now £3910 per week).

On other matters, objections from residents in Castle Road concerning the "Instow Project" (see April, 1987) had been received and Christian Contact had one hundred people who were involved as listeners or helpers, a hundred people had contacted the help-line and it was planned to man it twenty-four hours per day.

About the future building development, negotiations were still in progress with Sainsbury's regarding their plans to build a new superstore to the rear of the Coign Church property, with the possible inclusion of part of the land occupied by the Church.

At a Quarterly Church meeting held on 8 June 1989 it **Jun** was announced that Sean Larkin had formed a Church **1989** on Goldsworth Park (Lakeside Christian Fellowship), taking with him twenty Church members and David Brown had become a leader of a Church at Fareham under the oversight of Tony Morton. It had been agreed that Ray Booth would not resume leadership at the Coign and it was said that he planned to move back to Sheffield.

In September 1989 Sunday morning services **Sep** commenced at Woking 6th College, with evening **1989** meetings still being held at The Coign.

In November a Coign Fellowship report outlining the current leadership situation was produced and circulated. Howard Dodge, Brian Checksfield, Andrew Ryland and Mark Landreth Smith were meeting with Malcolm Kayes weekly with Howard responsible for taking final decisions. When Malcolm Kayes first became involved with the Church there had been no plans that this should continue once the way forward became clear; however, this possibility was being actively reconsidered. Howard then outlined his vision for the future:

- Find more suitable accommodation for the Sunday morning service as the 6th Form College was not ideal
- Give more attention to outreach
- Encourage discipleship of existing members
- Make prayer a matter of highest priority

During the last year the subject of ladies wearing head covering had been raised but as the Bible was not totally clear on the subject it was decided to let individual members make their own decisions on the matter.

Feb At a Church meeting held on 22 February 1990 it was **1990** reported that the Department of Environment had turned down the Church's request to erect Porta-cabins on the site. Later in September it was announced that Sainsbury's had withdrawn their offer for the purchase of the Church site.

At the Annual General Meeting held in April 1990 it **Apr** was reported that during the year twenty-nine people **1990** had been baptised and thirty-five came into membership, the total membership was five hundred and eighteen against five hundred and fifty-one the previous year, average weekly offerings were £3544 (down by £366), but missionary giving had increased by 80%.

Christian Contact had received five hundred calls in its first two years and over two hundred people had been helped. Mark Landreth Smith outlined a prophecy he and Howard had been given when they attended a conference at Holy Trinity Church, Brompton, London; Paul Cain, who knew little or nothing of towns in southern England said that he had a specific word for The Coign and Lakeside in Surrey - it was about repair and separation. Also, that Andrew was a peacemaker and Mark an evangelist. Soon after this prophecy Mark was relieved of his responsibilities

159

for the Young People's work and appointed as an Evangelist. Additionally, a meeting took place between Howard Dodge, Malcolm Kayes and Sean Larkin to bring some healing between the two Churches.

CHAPTER 9

GROWTH CONTINUES AND NEW PREMISES ARE NEEDED

Pastor: Malcolm Kayes 1991 to 1999 (and onwards to 2017)

Two significant events took place, one at the end of 1990 and the other at the beginning of 1991. On 13 **Dec** December 1990 a Special Church Meeting was held in **1990** line with the trust deeds and members were asked to consider the following motion "The Coign Fellowship invites Malcolm Kayes to be pastor of the Church". 85% of members were in favour and only 6% against (two hundred and eight and fifteen, with twenty-one abstentions). As a result, Malcolm Kayes was invited and subsequently took up his new position on 1 January 1991. Shortly afterwards, in January 1991, Sunday morning meetings were moved to Horsell High School.

Mar 1991 On 7 March 1991, with Malcolm Kayes officially in the chair for the first time at a Church Meeting, he announced that the emphasis for the coming months would be on cohesion and accountability. House Groups would meet fortnightly, leaving room for specific teaching on other subjects. The groups would have three main focus points:

- Towards God (worship and looking at his word).
- Towards each other (ministry and prayer).
- Towards the world (touching unbelievers).

The following month, at the Annual General Meeting, it was announced that Woking Borough Council had drawn up plans for a canal-side marina within the Vale Farm Road area, including the site of The Coign premises. Consequently, Mike Deavin was invited to investigate the possibility of The Coign moving to another site. Richard Wright spoke of Howard Dodge's official retirement on 31 July 1991. Howard would continue to work, receiving his pension and top up funding from the Church.

The Secretary reported that during the past year twenty-four people had been baptised and twenty come into membership. Overall membership was five hundred and one members compared with that of five hundred and eighteen the previous year. It was noted that the main hall at Horsell High School held five hundred and fifty and that the children were housed in a separate block. The treasurer announced that for the third year running there had been a decline in giving (10%).

On 3 July 1991, at a Church meeting, it was **Jul** announced that discussions concerning a possible new **1991** building were ongoing with Raymond Hall (architect) and a local builder. Amongst other matters it was reported that Mothers and Toddlers now had more than forty contacts; as a separate point, Malcolm Kayes said that he would prefer children to be older than twelve before being considered for baptism. It was proposed that the name of the Church should be changed to The Coign Church.

Oct On 2 October 1991 Mike Deavin reported that there
1991 had been no real progress with the building project, although discussions were still in progress concerning the St Peter's Convent site. The possibility of turning The Coign into a Museum for Woking was raised, but it was doubted that Woking Borough Council would have sufficient funding for the project.

At the same meeting it was announced that it had been decided not to hold House Groups from October through to early in the New Year. Instead, the time would be used to revitalise the leadership, re-evaluate the position of Elders, full time staff and House Group leaders. It was planned to appoint new Elders in due course.

On 18 February 1992 it was announced that Andrew **Feb**
Ryland would be starting a Just Looking Course for **1992**
those wishing to find out more about the Christian
faith. Howard Dodge pointed out that there had been
no baptisms for several months and that it was planned
that Nick Sharpe would become involved in
Wednesday Rendezvous as an outreach to those who
were not Christians. John Wardill said that three or
four people would be used for special care ministry.

A number of sites including that of Hall and Co,
which was located behind The Coign, between it and
the Basingstoke Canal, and St Peter's Convent,
Maybury were being considered for Church
development. Other sites, including The Pines, Skeet
and Jeff's and Victoria Hospital, were all suggested as
worth exploring.

At the Annual General Meeting held on 28 April 1992 **Apr**
it was reported that from 1 January 1992 the new **1992**
Eldership had been established (Malcolm Kayes,
Howard Dodge, Andrew Ryland, John Wardill and

Richard Wright). Nick Sharpe had taken on responsibility for the 'Way In', a drop in lunch club for the homeless and unemployed. During the year sixteen people had been baptised (twenty in 1990) and thirty-two had become Church members making up a total membership of four hundred and ninety-five (previously five hundred and one).

Giving had increased by 10% to £3511 per week and one third of this had been given away to a range of causes and people in need.

During the year seven hundred visitors had attended Sunday meetings.

Jul In July 1992 it was announced that J John would be
1992 holding a mission in Woking called Festival 94. (This was an inter-church enterprise with other events in the two years prior to the mission, starting with a video at Christchurch.) Nick Sharpe spoke about open air evangelism and Penny Sharpe reported that they had completed nine weeks of serving food, partially supplied by Marks & Spencer, to the homeless and out

of work on a Friday lunchtime ("Way in"); thirty non-Church people had attended, and twenty-two catering staff had helped. The children's mid-week groups, Warriors and Followers now had forty girls and thirty-seven boys. Unfortunately, no progress had been made with the building project.

On 14 October it was announced that Wednesday Rendezvous had re-commenced (after a short break) and thanks were expressed to Pat Bloomfield who had just given up its leadership. With regard to the building it had been decided to appoint an agent to look for possible sites. Malcolm Kayes outlined the Church's mission statement based on the word Coign:

- C = celebrate the uniqueness of Jesus Christ
- O = obey His call to discipleship and evangelism
- I = influence the town with the goodness of the gospel of Jesus Christ
- G = grow in size and quality in love and community
- N = nurture and care for one another

Feb On 3 February 1993 Nick Sharpe reported that there
1993 were now sixty-five people attending the "Way In".
Discussions with St Peter's Convent were not looking
hopeful and extending the existing Church buildings
was under consideration with a meeting with the
architect planned. An agent had been appointed to
investigate the possibility of finding commercial
buildings.

Apr At the Annual General Meeting held on 28 April
1993 1993, Malcolm Kayes reported that two building
possibilities were being considered. Firstly Ralph
Allen, the architect, had come to the Coign to see how
we could maximise the site and make provision for the
children's work. Unfortunately, his proposal was not
believed to be acceptable. Secondly whilst the
possible accommodation at St Peter's Convent had
been good there was no space to worship. It was noted
that Sunday morning meetings at Horsell High School
had continued during the year but that more space was

needed.

During the year thirteen people had been baptised and forty-five come into membership, making a total membership of four hundred and ninety-five. Between five hundred and five hundred and eighty people had attended Sunday morning meetings and two hundred and ninety to four hundred and one, Sunday evening meetings. Weekly offerings were now £3698 and there was a rise in direct missionary giving to £34,000. The income was now £284,383 (about the same as 1991).

Way In was going very well and approximately sixty people attended each week.

At a Church Meeting held on 30 June 1993 it was **Jun** reported that Christian Contact had received eighty **1993** calls, most of which were from people with emotional problems; three contacts had attended Coign Sunday services.

In October it was announced that it had been decided not to proceed with the St Peter's purchase primarily due to complicated procedures and financial structures.

On a more positive note five houses in Oaks Road, currently owned by Sainsbury's had come onto the market at a cost of £170,000. If the Church was interested in purchasing these, a bid was required by 28 October and Woking Borough Council had agreed that they would give a two-year temporary change of use licence for these buildings to be used as classrooms and offices. The properties in Oaks Road were in a poor state of repair and would require significant refurbishment.

Richard Wright reported on the unemployment meetings (twelve non-Christians had been involved). Nick Sharpe reported that Way In had been running now for eighteen months (sixty to seventy attendees), and that a Just Looking course was running in West End.

Mar 1994 At a Special Church Meeting, held on 1 March 1994, at which two hundred were present, it was reported that an offer of £210,000 had been made and accepted for 9, 13, 15, 17 and 23 Oaks Road. 5 Oaks Road was already owned by the Coign and investigations were under way concerning numbers 7 and 11. The overall purpose of purchasing these buildings was to a) meet the current need for Sunday and children's work, and b) provide counselling and administration accommodation. Completion was expected by the end of May. In the longer term the intention was to obtain as much adjacent land as possible so that the main meeting area of The Coign could be extended. To raise the necessary finance, it was decided to hold a gift day on 20 March.

It was also mentioned that there was a possibility that two Sunday morning meetings at The Coign may be the way forward.

At the Annual General Meeting, held on 29 March **Mar** 1994, it was announced that the Church's Trust deed **1994** had been altered concerning a change of name; The Coign Fellowship had now officially become The Coign Church.

During the year twenty-seven people had been baptised and thirty-one come into membership making a total membership of four hundred and ninety-four. At a head count on a Sunday five hundred and twenty-four people were present at the morning service and three hundred in the evening. Weekly offerings had reached £3727 per week but overall there was a deficit in income, at the end of the year, of £15,000.

No further news was available concerning the availability of 7 and 11 Oaks Road.

Andrew Ryland was leaving to lead the Runneymede Church and was to be replaced on the staff by John Wardill.

There was only eighteen days before the start of 'Festival '94'; forty-three thousand leaflets were about to be distributed around the town; and it was proposed that the Church hold a barn dance, a 60/70's night, a golf day and a cabaret. The Church secretary reported that the supply of free food from Marks & Spencer for the Way In work had stopped and that weekly attendance had increased to between sixty and one hundred people.

At a Church Meeting held on 28 June 1994 it was **Jun** announced that change of use had been officially **1994** granted by Woking Borough Council for the new premises, no alterations were to be made to 17 Oaks Road (and this was subsequently let out) and there was no further news concerning numbers 7 and 11. Overall there was still a deficit of £30,000 following the acquisition of the Oaks Road properties.

It had been decided to stop holding Sunday morning meetings at Horsell High School with the final Sunday service being held on 17 July. With effect from August, Sunday meetings would be held back at The Coign and from 4 September there would be two morning meetings (09:00 and 10:45).

With regard to Church planting, a meeting was to be arranged with Dave Holden from New Frontiers International to discuss the possibility of the Church taking over an existing Church on the Old Dean Estate in Camberley with Mark Landreth-Smith possibly leading the work.

Oct 1994 On 9 October 1994 it was announced that £16,000 was still needed for the building project completion (to date receipts totalled £256,460, £250,300 having been paid out) with the remaining amount required for refurbishment. Mike Deavin announced that the new buildings would be called "The Acorn Centre".

Two Sunday morning services had taken place for each of the previous five weeks.

Mark Landreth-Smith had started membership classes in Camberley and it was anticipated that the new Church, called the Beacon Church, would start in the New Year under Mark's leadership.

Towards the end of 1994, the Church experienced a

period of what was known as "The Toronto Blessing"[6] that continued for the following twelve to eighteen months. It was different from other times when the Holy Spirit had moved on the Church. People were affected in a variety of ways from laughter, falling down and resting in God, to singing, praising and shaking. There was, without doubt, a clear sense of the presence of God and the Father's love upon all. Many were blessed and felt a renewal and closeness in their relationship with the Lord.

On 25 January 1995 it was reported that 17 Oaks Road **Jan** was ready for occupation; the Sunday Children's **1995**

---

6 "The Toronto Blessing is a term coined by British Churches to describe the revival and resulting phenomena that began in January 1994 at Toronto Airport Vineyard Christian Fellowship, now known as Toronto Airport Christian Fellowship (TACF), a neocharismatic evangelical Christian Church located in Toronto, Ontario, Canada.. Participants in the conferences and meetings sponsored by TACF have reported healings, incidents of personal transformation and a greater awareness of God's love. It has also been referred to as The Father's Blessing, The Anointing, The Awakening, The River, and The Fire" (http://en.wikipedia.org/wiki/Toronto_Blessing).

work, under the leadership of Lynne Newman, had one hundred and ten three-to-twelve-year olds in the first service and fifty in the second. The Beacon Church at Camberley had seventy attending during the initial weeks.

Two hundred and seventy-five chairs had been ordered to replace the pews in the chapel area of the Coign.

Mar 1995 At the Annual General Meeting in March 1995, it was reported that the Beacon Church had officially opened on Easter Sunday and 80 people had attended the service.

With regard to the building plans there was a possibility that the Church building and land would be subject to compulsory purchase by Woking Borough Council and the Church possibly moved to a new site opposite Peacocks, the new town-centre shopping centre.

During the last year twenty-eight people had been baptised, thirty-one had come into membership making a total membership of four hundred and ninety-three, average Sunday attendance was three hundred and five (first service) and two hundred and seventy-six (second service) and in the evening two hundred and sixty six. Offerings were over £4000 per week (reaching the sum received prior to the Chertsey plantout).

At the Quarterly Church Meeting held on 25 October **Oct** 1995 it was announced that the Church had received a **1995** letter from Woking Borough Council stating that the move of the Church to a new site had been temporarily deferred for financial reasons.

At the Annual General Meeting in March 1996 it was **Mar** announced that a new work with the older young **1996** people would start shortly; it would be called Blaze and would replace the existing group named Breakthrough. Lynne Newman had decided to cease leading the Children's work and as a result Hazel Pearce had agreed to co-ordinate activities.

Mid-week attendees had been studying a discipleship

book and it was decided to stop this activity and place more emphasis on working with the community. The gospel presentation play "Heaven's Gates and Hell's Flames" was in the planning stages to be performed during November 1996 and sixty members would be needed to participate.

There were currently three options for building development now that the Council had decided not to pursue their plans to re-develop Vale Farm Road:

- Redevelop the Coign site.
- Obtain further properties in Oaks Road and build on an enlarged site.
- Build new premises on a totally new site.

Oct 1996 On 1 October 1996 it was reported that the children on a Sunday morning would be following a new syllabus as it was often difficult to keep to the topics covered by the main congregation. Initially it would be for a year, but then extended to three years if it worked well.

The Beacon Church, Camberley, was looking to re-develop their building or move to a school and use the existing premises during the week. Alpha, the introduction to Christianity course developed at Holy Trinity, Brompton, would start at The Coign in January 1997.

Woking Borough Council had encouraged the Church to submit a planning application to extend the current Church buildings.

On 18 March 1997, at the Annual General Meeting, it **Mar** was announced that Baptismal services had been held **1997** on eight occasions with seventeen people being baptised and that thirty-seven people had come into membership making a total membership of five hundred and two. On average approximately three hundred and twenty attended the first Sunday morning service, two hundred and fifty the second and two hundred and ninety-seven the evening service.

Malcolm Kayes announced that Alan Hunwicks was soon to become an Elder. In the summer of 1996, five hundred had attended a Bible week held at Stoneleigh Agricultural Showground organised by New Frontiers International.

With regard to other developments it was noted that Geoff Owers had recently retired as Church Treasurer; sincere thanks were expressed to Geoff for his faithful service since 1969.

Thirty-five had attended the first Alpha course and due to the success of the first performance, provisional arrangements were in progress to hold a second performance of 'Heaven's Gates and Hell's Flames' at the HG Wells Centre in Woking.

With regard to the building project it was reported that contracts had been exchanged for the purchase of 11 Oaks Road with a move of the occupants to 23. No 7 was still owned privately.

The treasurer reported that there had been a 5% growth in giving during the past year. Looking back over twenty-five years to 1972 when Sunday offerings were £100 per week and it was a 'one-man ministry', now there were ten full time staff, we had suffered substantial inflation but only once gone into the red (£80,000 for the 1975 land purchase, although the debt had been finally cleared prior to moving into the new Church building). On 1 July 1997 it was announced **Jul** that 11 Oaks Road had finally been purchased and that **1997** there was interest in developing the Vale Farm area; Steve Brading, a leader in the New Frontiers Church in Hastings, would be visiting The Coign during April.

At the Annual General Meeting held on 31 March **Mar** 1998 it was reported that during the previous twelve **1998** months there had been thirty-eight baptisms, and nineteen new members, making a total of four hundred and ninety-nine members.

An approach to purchase 7 Oaks Road had been made, but not accepted. There had been a number of bids for the Church site and in general these were favourable. An approach to Woking Borough Council had been made concerning the possibility of the Coign Church building new premises on the Brewery Road car park.

Jul 1998 On 1 July 1998 it was announced that Jeremy Bunce would be joining the full-time staff on 1 September 1998 as a pastoral worker. Steve Brading was to join, too, on 1 January 1999.

Sep 1998 On 29 September 1998 it was reported that the possibility of selling The Coign site was still under consideration and a full report would be available soon.

Karen Pugh spoke of the special needs' group she had run at Runnymede Church and the decision to set up a similar support group at The Coign.

Mar 1999 At the Annual General Meeting held in March 1999 it was announced that there would be a new structure for the midweek discipleship groups which had been meeting since 1994, each with between twelve and sixteen members. Faith for multiplication of these groups was sought. A vision statement for the Church was also presented to members.

> ### *Vision statement*
>
> *'We seek to be an Antioch Church that equips and releases our members to Kingdom ministry and mission, a recognised local Christian community 'meeting people's real needs with God's real power', and a house of prayer for all nations.'*

At the end of 1999 there were five hundred and thirty-one members (thirty-two more than the previous year).

At a Church Meeting held on 3 December 1999 it was **Dec** announced that the Building Group were still looking **1999** for possible new sites for the Church premises. They had looked at the town centre, Brookwood Chapel, a greenfield site in Worplesdon as well as the possibility of remaining at the present site. Outline planning permission for building on the Brewery Road car park would be submitted soon.

Appendix D, Figures 19 and 20 show the Coign building exterior and interior.

Chapter 10

EPILOGUE

Looking back over the years since 1879 there have been many seasons of outstanding blessing experienced by members of our Church. Many of these occurred well before I was born. However, even in my lifetime I am thankful to God for being present during the outpouring of the Holy Spirit in the Coffee Bar during the late 1960s and then more widely in the years immediately following. How could anybody who lived through the "mountain experience" forget the amazement of seeing God at work? Then there have been numerous times when we have met as a Church on a Sunday or mid-week when God has really made Himself known to us.

In contrast there have also been other times, such as during the early days of the Church's development when the path has been far from smooth and dedication and perseverance in the Christian walk have been required.

However, whether in blessing or in periods of testing God has been actively building His Church in Woking. Much more could be said but I will end with this quote from Matthew 16 v 18:

"I will build my Church and the gates of Hell shall not prevail against it".

References

Baptist Churches in Surrey (1909),
edited by AH Stockwell, London. Pages 248 to 250.
History of Woking, Ryde, E. (1883). Manuscript at Surrey History Centre.
Woking 150 – The history of Woking and its Railway,
Wakeford, I. (1987) The Mayford and District History Society.

APPENDIX A

LEST WE FORGET

Introduction

A search of the records held by the Surrey History Centre and other sources was undertaken by Richard and Rosemary Christophers and the current author to see if further information about the individuals named on three memorial wall plaques, subsequently mounted at Woking Baptist Church, could be found (Appendix D, Figure 12).

Church members saw active service in both the First and Second World Wars. Fourteen names are given of those who died between 1914 and 1918 and four who died between 1939 and 1945.

With a few exceptions, the part that each played in Church life has not been possible to establish. Only God knows the depth of their relationship and commitment to him.

The remainder of this Appendix documents what is known about the individual Church members who gave their lives for their country.

WORLD WAR ONE

Charles Ernest Bessant

Charles was born on 24 March 1895 in Chertsey [St Peter's Hospital was not built then: he was baptised into the Church of England at St Peter's Church, Chertsey]. He attended Maybury School, belonged to the Christ Church Woking company of the C. L. B. and was a member of the Bible Class football team. His father was a railway porter and Charles followed him into the railway where he became a signal lad. To better himself he resigned from this position on 29 May 1912.

Charles joined the 2nd Battalion of the Grenadier Guards in November 1913, was awarded the rank of Lance Corporal and subsequently made up to a full Corporal. Shortly after the outbreak of war he was posted to the front, and he served throughout the beginning of the campaign without a scratch and without receiving a day's leave.

However, he died, aged 20, on 12 October 1915 at Flanders, Belgium. He was killed by a shell bursting in the trench he was occupying.

Charles Edward John ("Chick") Evitt

Charles was born in Girlington, Bradford, Yorkshire on 25 September 1888. He came from a family of photographers. In May 1907 he joined the Post Office at Chertsey, Surrey. The records show that he served as a general servant on RMS "Athenic" departing from London for Wellington, New Zealand and then on various ships sailing to and from Wellington as a general servant or steward.

Charles is named in New Zealand World War 1 reserve Army rolls as a storeman in 1916-17 and also as a waiter. He died from influenza on 28 November and was buried two days later in the Karori Cemetery, New Zealand. His mother lived at 10 The Broadway, Woking, at the time of his death.

William George Fletcher

William was born in the first quarter of 1898 and was one of four brothers who served with the forces. He joined the Royal Army Medical Corps and was attached to 1st Battalion Kings Shropshire Light Infantry. He died, age 19, at the end of 1917 and was buried in the Marcoing Communal Cemetery in northern France.

The Woking News and Mail (21 December 1917) and the Surrey Advertiser (22 December 1917) record that William had a strong sense of duty to his country, our cause and to God; he had strong principles and joined RAMC especially that he might be useful ministering to suffering men in the name of Christ. One tribute, recorded in the News and Mail (22 February 1918), had been sent to his parents from an officer in a London Hospital whose wounds William had dressed under gunfire "without regard to his own safety" and said that he had also tended him at Loos and Cambrai. "A lovely Christian life".

Henry William Gloster

Henry, also known as Harry, was educated at Ryde House School, Ripley and afterwards joined the staff of Messrs HW Gloster and Sons. He was the son of one of the founding Church members and played an active part in Church life.

On the outbreak of war, he enlisted in the City of London Royal Fusiliers, with whom he served in Egypt and Gallipoli. He was one of three men wounded in the evacuations of the Peninsula. After spending six months in France he came home with septic poisoning. On recovering he then transferred to the Tanks, with whom he served for some 14 months. He was wounded in the leg and foot, subsequently re-joined his unit and was gassed. Pneumonia supervened with fatal results. Harry died, aged 25 years old, on 8 October 1918 and was buried in Mont Huon Military Cemetery, Le Treport, France.

Stephen William Hayter

Stephen was baptised on 4 December 1898 at Christ Church, Woking. He joined the Army Machine Gun Corps 3rd Battalion as a Private. He died, aged 19, at the 3rd Battle of Albert on 21 August 1918. He is buried in the Bucquoy Cemetery, Northern France.

Percy Holder

Percy was born in Surrey on 14 July 1882 and emigrated to Canada in 1908, joining the 54th Kootenay Bn, CEF, aged 33, on 13 August 1915. He served in France where his profession is listed as bomber and wirer.

In early 1916 Percy was admitted to the Aldershot Isolation Hospital with suspected rubella but returned to France shortly afterwards. It appears that he was subsequently wounded, around September 1916 and died at the end of the year or beginning of 1917. His name is noted on the Vimy War Memorial in Pas de Calais and on his family grave at Peach Orchard Cemetery, British Columbia, Canada.

Harry Horace Jater

Harry, the son of a painter, was baptised on 18 March 1885 and was a pupil at Board School Road, Woking. His father was a grocer's porter. He joined the Essex Regiment, 4th Battalion, and served as a private in Palestine where he died at the capture of Gaza. His name is recorded on the Jerusalem Memorial.

The News and Mail (7 December 1917) and The Surrey Advertiser (8 December 1917) recorded his death in an article headed "Religious worker killed". They note that Harry was a member of the Baptist Church and was well known in this district as a local preacher and an earnest social worker. Among other offices, he held that of superintendent of the Courtenay Road Sunday School and he did good work among the van dwellers at Kingfield and elsewhere.

Gilbert Paul Macdonald

Gilbert's role as Choirmaster at Woking Baptist Church has been given in an earlier section of this book and is not repeated here. Details of his son's death in the Second World War are recorded later in this Appendix.

Gilbert was the fourth son of Peter Macdonald. He joined the army on 10 December 1915 and served in the Reserve Force on the Home Front and then as a Private in the 1/15th Regiment (Prince of Wales's Own, Civil Service Battalion). He was posted to France on 13 August 1917 and served as a rifleman.

Initially he was reported missing during a counterattack on Cambrai (northern France) at the end of November 1917. His death was subsequently confirmed as 28 November 1917. He was 33 years old when he died.

A letter from his Colonel stated that he was shot in the head and killed instantly The Surrey Advertiser (8 April 1918) in an article about Gilbert recorded that he was "a jolly companion and did his duty to the last".

David Waters Orr

David was born in 1881 and worked as a postman for 16 years prior to his call up to serve in the army. A year prior to the start of his military service he married Claire, a Chatham lady, in Rochester Cathedral.

He joined the London Regiment Post Office Rifles in March 1916 and was drafted overseas on 24 October 1916. He served in Belgium and died whilst on active service on 28 August 1917. His name is recorded on the Menin Gate Memorial in Belgium.

Herbert Provins and Arthur Provins

Herbert and Arthur Edward Provins both served and died during the first World War; the first in France aged 24, on 13 May 1915 and the second, aged 19, on 31 May 1916.

Herbert was born in 1890. He joined the army and served in the Hampshire Regiment 1st Battalion and is remembered on the Menin Gate, Ypres, Belgium. He was killed four months from enlisting and ten days after leaving England.

Arthur Edward was born on 28 May 1897 and joined the Royal Navy at the age of 15 and trained on the HMS "Warspite". He then served on the maiden voyage of the

HMS "Queen Mary". In his last letter to his mother he wrote that he was well.

He was killed at the Battle of Jutland when his ship was hit twice by the German battleship "Derfflinger" and its magazines exploded, sinking the ship. The wreck rests on the floor of the North Sea and was discovered in 1991. It is the grave of about 1266 officers and men; there were only 20 survivors.

Edwin Reed

Edwin enlisted in the army in 1900 and served for seven years in India before being transferred to the Reserve. Subsequently he entered the employ of Mr WG Tarrant, builder (the Surrey Advertiser 8 April 1916).

He was called up on the outbreak of war and he took part in several engagements in France, including Neuve Chapelle and afterwards proceeded to Mesopotamia, where his battery was attached to General Aylmer's Relief Force. At the time of his death he was a gunner in the Royal Field Artillery 19th Battery in Basra, Iraq.

Edwin was connected with the Woking Baptist Church and was generally respected.

Herbert Snell and Norris Snell

Herbert and Norris were brothers and dentists who served in the army.

Herbert was born on 16 June 1880 and died on 7 April 1917, age 36. He was educated at Guy's Hospital where he qualified as a dentist in 1906. He had a dental practice in Woking, Surrey, until he joined the Inns of Court O.T.C. in 1916. Shortly after enrolment he was posted to the front line in France and served as a 2nd Lieutenant in 24th Battalion London Regiment, attached 2nd /6th Battalion Lancashire Fusiliers. He was killed while returning from patrol duty, for which he had volunteered. His grave is in Brown's Road Military Cemetery, Festubert, France. The Surrey Advertiser (23 April 1917) and Woking News and Mail (20 April 1917) record that Herbert was greatly liked and esteemed by all who knew him, professionally or otherwise.

Norris was born on 25 March 1875 and his story is given in the De Ruvigny Roll of Honour from Ancestry: "Norris held a commission in the 1st Suffolk and Harwich R. G. A. for some time. He volunteered his services on the outbreak of war in August 1914. He was gazetted Lieutenant East Yorkshire Regiment on 3 December 1914 and promoted to Captain in April 1915. He served with the Expeditionary Force in France and Flanders from August 1915. He was severely wounded in the chest, neck and arm at Loos in September 1915. He re-joined his regiment in February 1916, returning to France in March and was killed in action at Longueval on 14 July and buried at Bazentin-le-Grand. His major wrote "He and I were always so friendly, and he used to work so hard and cheerfully always getting his men to do the same, that he will ever be remembered in this battalion. I am glad to say he met his end from a bullet instantaneously at the head of his men, leading them on".

WORLD WAR TWO

Douglas Alexander Hutcheson Allan

Douglas was born on 9 July 1917 and died 25 March 1941. He served in the Royal Navy on the SS "Britannia". His ship was bound from the United Kingdom to India when she was intercepted by the German raider "Thor", 720 miles west of Freetown. There was an unequal action for over an hour, the liner putting up a stout fight with her single gun. At the end of this time she was compelled to stop and lower her boats. The "Thor" then sank her by gunfire but made no attempt to help survivors. Later one boat containing 63 persons was picked up by the Spanish steamer "Bachi" and another with 38 persons reached Brazil after a voyage of 23 days. Of the 203 crew and 281 passengers, 122 of the crew and 127 passengers lost their lives. Douglas did not survive the attack.

David Rowlands Dimmick

David was born in Lymington on 1 August 1912 and died, age, 28 on 26/27 April 1941. He served in the Royal Army Service Corps, 308 Res MT Company.

In April 1941 the War Office initially recorded, that Sergeant David Dimmick was presumed lost and subsequently as lost by enemy action at sea. He was 28 years of age and was the son of Rev F T Dimmick formerly minister at Kingfield Baptist Church. Sergeant Dimmick was involved with the evacuation from Greece.

Hamish Wheeler Macdonald

Hamish was born in 1918 and was the son of Gilbert Paul Macdonald (see page 192).

He joined the Royal Air Force Volunteer Reserve 149 Squadron. The squadron was a photographic reconnaissance unit flying Blenheim aircraft. At the time of his death they were changing from Blenheims to Venturas. The Surrey Advertiser (8 May 1943) records that Hamish died in a flying accident.

Gilbert Peter Rowe

Gilbert attended the Woking County School for Boys. He attained Colours for rugby, football (1st X1 1936), senior cricket team and was a member of Woking Swimming

Club. On leaving school he joined Martin's Bank in Lombard Street London.

He was a Sergeant Observer in the 59th Squadron of the Royal Air Force and was reported as missing on the 26 July 1940.

APPENDIX B

DEVELOPMENT OF MUSIC IN OUR WORSHIP

(Tony Lyttle writes from the historical records and his own and Alice Potter's contemporary recollections)

Singing as part of the Church's worship crops up in Church records as early as 1881, when hymnbooks were purchased – and rented to Church members to recoup the outlay! At that time the Sunday School Superintendent, John Ashley, agreed to lead the singing. His role would have been that of a precentor who 'raised the tunes,' that is, started off the songs in the right key for the congregation to follow. By 1884 the Church had acquired an 'organ' of some sort – possibly a harmonium – but they definitely had an organist.

The importance of music was recognised in 1892 when a musical committee was established to guide its use in the services and in 1901 Gilbert McDonald became 'organist and choirmaster' – a position he held for the next 16 years. So, by that date the Church also had a choir to lead the singing. In 1911 it was decided to upgrade their 'organ' and another was purchased from Hastings for £195. In January 1915 copies of the Baptist Church Hymnal were first introduced for congregational singing.

When the new Church building was being planned for Percy Street, in 1925, the sum of £500 was set aside for the erection of a full pipe organ in the new premises. In 1945 the choir was re-formed as a 'Christian choir' (what it had been previously was not explained.) A decade later, in 1955, it was decided that the choir shouldn't sing an anthem during the service but rather be like the choirs leading the worship at the Billy Graham Haringey rallies.

It was about this time that Barry Potter became the Church organist, a position that he held until the Church left the building in 1976 *en route* to their new premises at The Coign. Before vacating Percy Street, Barry didn't want to see the splendid organ end up on a scrapheap and he undertook to advertise it, worldwide, for sale at a reasonable price in order to try to ensure a purchaser. It was bought by the owner of an Organ Museum in Canberra, Australia. This man's son was in England and came and helped Barry dismantle the pipe organ piece by piece. All the parts were packed into crates which were then shipped off to the other side of the world where they were re-built and installed in the Canberra Organ Museum.

Back in 1958, a few years after Barry Potter started at the Church, Philip Jones became pastor and introduced the use of the Keswick Hymnal, on a trial basis, for Sunday morning communion services, but in 1962 it was decided to purchase further copies of the Baptist Church Hymnal so the trial must not have been a success.

The Church followed the traditional style of service with a four-hymn sandwich. This continued throughout the time of Philip Jones and on to his successor, Harold Owen. It was during Harold's ministry that the movement of the Holy Spirit began to revitalise His people, and this became particularly evident in our times of worship.

New inspired songs were being written which we mainly learned through the annual Bible Weeks at Capel, the Dales and the Downs from a plethora of new music books such as, *Youth Praise, Worship in Song, Renewal in Song, Scripture in Song, Songs of Fellowship* and *Sound of Living Waters*. Often these were scripture choruses with simple melodies that were easy to pick up and had the ability to lift the congregation to new heights of worship as we praised our heavenly Father and experienced, in return, His Holy Spirit ministering to us through the words and music. They were also an excellent way to learn the scriptures and have them embedded within our memories. (How many of us, who experienced those times, can still recite the nine-fold fruit of the Spirit as the names appeared in the chorus rather than in the order in which Paul lists them in Galatians?)

During this period the old Baptist hymnbook was replaced by the Redemption Hymnal which, it was agreed, contained a better selection of livelier hymns. These were used alongside the modern choruses. The change was not without its objectors, however, and for quite a while the old Baptist Hymnal was retained for use in the morning services. The organ continued to be played, too, on Sunday mornings, but the evening services, which included much longer times of singing and worship, soon found Barry out of his organ loft and providing accompaniment on the grand piano that had been purchased for the production of the Wondrous Story radio programmes each week.

Prior to the commencement of the service Barry would play a selection of choruses and it was often said that the service actually started before the Elders arrived on the platform as people were already singing along with these choruses. After an opening welcome, the service proper would normally start with an extended time of worship led by one of the Elders who would announce the first song. Usually, as the worship time continued, people would feel inspired to pray out from the congregation; someone else would start another chorus. Then, perhaps someone would pray in tongues and another would bring the interpretation under the inspiration of the Holy Spirit. Another song would be started up or someone would read a passage of scripture that was on their heart, and so it continued.

Time and time again we marvelled at how what appeared to be disparate contributions actually complimented one another, dovetailing together to present a theme, both in words and in songs; a theme which was often reflected in the sermon that the preacher had already prepared to bring that evening. As the Holy Spirit is allowed free reign His ways are wonderful to behold.

Barry was an excellent organist and pianist who could read and play any piece of music set before him. He did not, however, play by ear and this presented him with a problem when choruses were started from the congregation which would not necessarily be in the key in which they were written in Barry's music books. But when, along with so many of us at that time, Barry was first filled with the Holy Spirit he found that, miraculously, he could now play the tunes by ear and, if necessary transpose the music into the correct key if they had been started too low or too high.

A guitarist would sometimes lead the worship and other instrumentalists began to take their place around the piano to enhance the sound. We usually had a clarinet, flute and violin with occasionally some brass, too – trumpet, tuba – and we even had a xylophone for a while.

When we moved to The Coign, now called The Welcome Centre, Barry always played the grand piano as there was no organ at The Coign. The worship leader was usually a guitarist, who would lead from the front, while other instrumentalists occupied the side pews near the piano.

Shortly after the move to our new premises, The Coign Fellowship, as we were then known produced its own song book of many of the new choruses that we were singing as well as some golden oldies. 'For His Praise' contained 275 scripture choruses and other songs, many of which had arisen out of the recent move of the Holy Spirit. This served us well for a few years until there were just too many 'even newer' songs to be accommodated and we started to use acetates on an overhead projector. (Their eventual replacement, in an electronic age, by the computerised "SongPro" will no doubt be covered in some future volume of our Church Story.)

When Malcolm Kayes became Pastor, he often led the worship himself, playing his guitar. The informal group of instrumentalists were formed into a regular band which Alice and Barry led and co-ordinated. The side pews were removed to make proper space for the players and their instruments, including a full set of drums and an electronic keyboard that Barry played, with Alice on the grand piano.

Church on the Move covers the Church's story up to 1999 and it was about then, or just shortly afterwards, that Barry retired as Church Organist. I don't know if his title was ever officially changed to Church Pianist! – but he did end up back on an organ, albeit an electronic one. His 45 or so years in office had overseen the most radical changes in style and use of music in our worship in the whole of our Church's history. The transition from staid, traditional hymn sandwich to open and free worship where anything may happen, and often did, could not always have been easy for him. But Barry, a humble Christian and true gentleman, was happy to accommodate whatever God was doing in His Church; to go with the flow and to – yes – just, play it by ear.

As a Church, we were experiencing – many, perhaps, for the first time – what true, Spirit-inspired worship really is.

APPENDIX C

BAPTISMS AND CHURCH MEMBERSHIP STATISTICS

One of the ways of assessing Church growth has been to summarise the number of people who have become Christians, been baptised and officially joined the Church each year. This information has been reported at the Annual General Church meeting held each Spring and is summarised overleaf. There are gaps in the record, either completely missing years or where only partial data is available. However, the data clearly show periods of growth and years when numbers decreased. For example, membership had dropped to twenty-eight active members in 1897 and, as a consequence, Edward Tarbox was invited to return to lead the Church. Subsequently the numbers increased. In contrast, there were years of significant and sustained growth in the 1980s and 1990s when membership rose to five hundred and fifty in 1985 and remained around this number for many years. Baptisms reached a maximum of ninety-five in 1985. This period of growth took place primarily under Harold Owen's and Malcom Kayes' ministries during the "out-pouring of the Holy Spirit", described in the main body of this book.

MEMBERSHIP AND BAPTISMS			
Year	Members	Baptisms	Comments
1879	8		
1883	43		+ 24 members at Knaphill
1884	70		Includes members who attended Knaphill
1897		8	First baptisms
1891	68		
1895	82		
1897	28		+4 Associates +5 Honorary
1900	96		After analysis of communion attendance 69 active members

MEMBERSHIP AND BAPTISMS			
Year	Members	Baptisms	Comments
1906			14 became Christians following 4-day mission. 39 joined the Church (19 became Christians + 20 transfers in)
1913	133		+ 30 honorary members
1914	152		
1916	164		+ 26 honorary members
1917	195		
1918	204		
1934	350		
1951	67		
1967	107		> this number
1968	240/ 221		
1971	250		20 baptised, 11 new members
1972	270		
1973	275		
1976		44	Base number not known but there were 52 new members
1977		51	36 new members
1978		40	36 new members
1981	370	63	46 new members
1983		91	126 new members

MEMBERSHIP AND BAPTISMS			
Year	Members	Baptisms	Comments
1985	550	92	85 new members
1987		60	73 new members
1988	631	48	60 new members (41 transfers, 160 left including 72 to the new Church plant in Chertsey and 43 moving away)
1989	531	45	> 45 new members - 19 of whom were new Christians
1990	518	29	35 new members
1991	501	24	21 new members
1992	495	16	32 New members
1993	495	13	45 new members
1994	494	27	31 new members
1995	493	28	31 new members (A significant group left to be part of the new Church plant in Camberley)
1997	502	17	37 new members
1998	499	38	19 new members
1999	531		

APPENDIX D

IMAGES

Figure 1. Woking in the 1870's

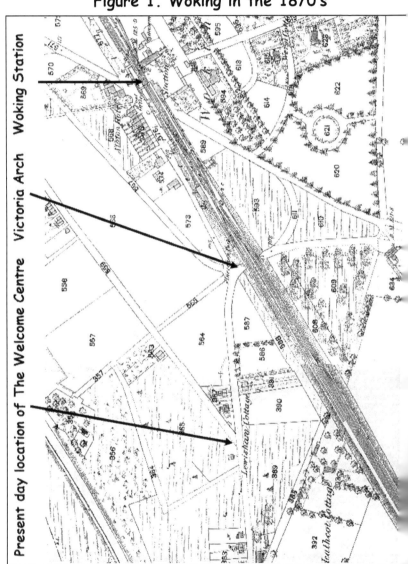

Figure 2. Woking in 1896

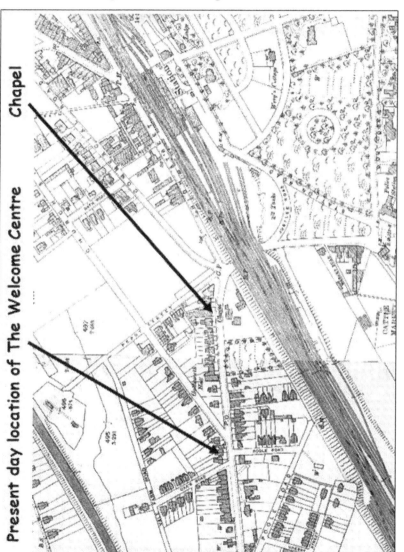

Figure 3. Woking in 1912

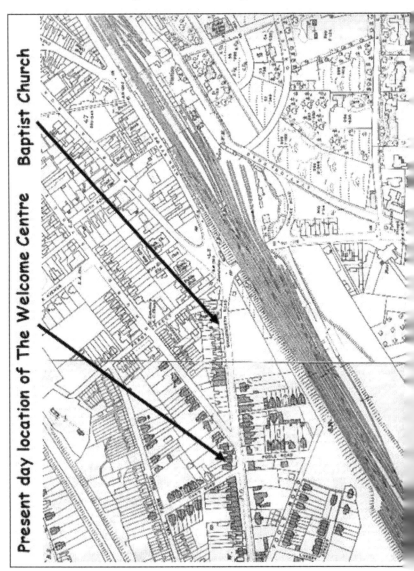

Figure 4. Woking in 1934

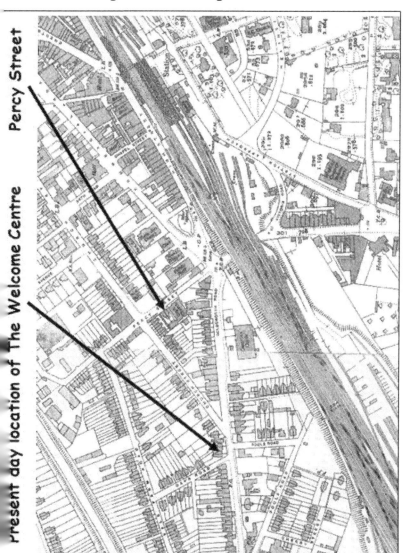

John Gloster

Figure 5 Henry William Gloster

Figure 6. Sketch plan of the first Church building

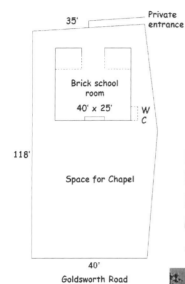

35'

Private entrance

Brick school room

40' x 25'

W
C

118'

Space for Chapel

40'

Goldsworth Road

Figure 7. Goldsworth Road Baptist Church building.
Photo by permission, Alvina Gould

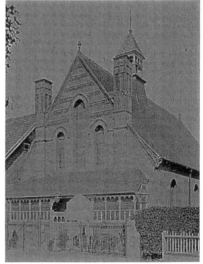

Figure 8. Order of Service for the Foundation Stone Laying Ceremony for Percy Street Baptist Church, 1924

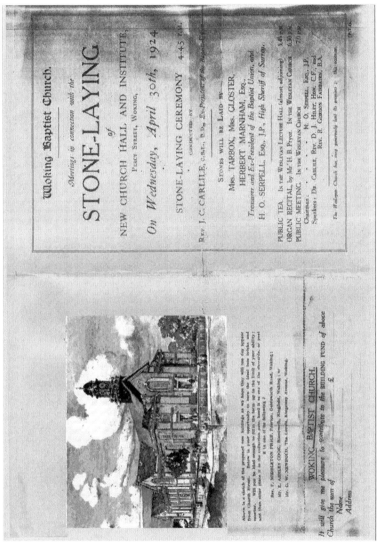

Figure 9. Order of Service for the Foundation Stone Laying Ceremony (inside)

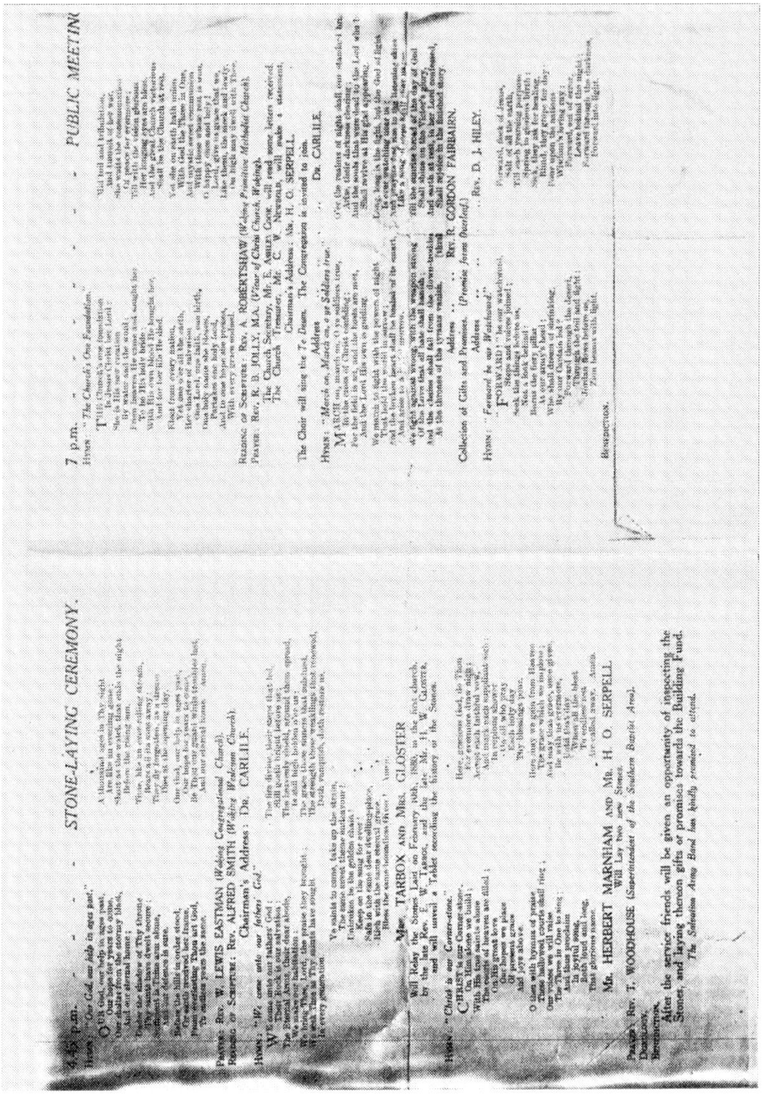

4.45 p.m. - - - - STONE-LAYING CEREMONY.

Hymn: "Our God, our help in ages past."

Prayer: Rev. W. LEWIS EASTMAN (Woking Congregational Church).
Reading of Scripture: Rev. ALFRED SMITH (Woking Wesleyan Church).

Chairman's Address: Dr. CARLILE.

Hymn: "We come unto our fathers' God."

Mrs. TARBOX and Mrs. GLOSTER

Will Relay the Stones Laid on February 19th, 1880, in the first church, by the late Rev. E. W. Tarbox, and the late Mr. H. W. Gloster, and will unveil a Tablet recording the history of the Stones.

Hymn: "Christ is our Corner-stone."

Mr. HERBERT MARNHAM and Mr. H. O. SERPELL
Will Lay two new Stones.

Prayer: Rev. T. WOODHOUSE (Superintendent of the Southern Baptist Area).
Doxology.
Benediction.

After the service friends will be given an opportunity of inspecting the Stones, and laying thereon gifts or promises towards the Building Fund.

The Salvation Army Band has kindly promised to attend.

7 p.m. - - - - PUBLIC MEETING

Hymn: "The Church's One Foundation."

Reading of Scripture: Rev. A. ROBERTSHAW (Woking Primitive Methodist Church).
Prayer: Rev. R. B. JOLLY, M.A. (Vicar of Christ Church, Woking).

The Church Secretary, Mr. E. Ashley Cave, will read some letters received.
The Church Treasurer, Mr. C. V. Newman, will make a statement.

Chairman's Address: Mr. H. O. SERPELL.

The Choir will sing the Te Deum. The Congregation is invited to join.

Address . . Dr. CARLILE.

Hymn: "March on, March on, o ye Soldiers true."

Address . . Rev. R. GORDON FAIRBAIRN.

Collection of Gifts and Promises. (Promise forms Overleaf.)

Address . . Rev. D. J. HILEY.

Hymn: "Forward be our Watchword."

Benediction.

Figure 10. Percy Street Baptist from an original sketch by Chas Davis

Figure 11. Baptist Church building on Percy Street. Photo by permission, Alvina Gould

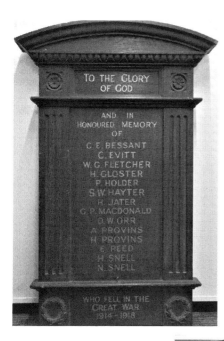

**Figure 12.
Commemorative
plaques remembering
the slain of our
Church in the two
World Wars**

Figure 13. Monthly Church magazine from 1924

FORWARD.

The Monthly Magazine

—— OF THE ——

WOKING BAPTIST CHURCH.

GOLDSWORTH ROAD, WOKING.   ANTHONY'S, HORSELL.

VOL. I.   NOVEMBER, 1924.   No. 11.

DIARY.

SUNDAY—

Morning Service at 11 a.m.
Sunday School at 3 p.m.
Bible Classes at 3 p.m.
Evening Service at 6.30 p.m.
Communion Service at Evening Service 1st
    Sunday, Morning Service 3rd Sunday.

MONDAY—

Band of Hope and Juvenile Rechabite Tent
    at 6.30 p.m.

TUESDAY—

Church Sewing Meeting at 3 p.m.

WEDNESDAY—

Mutual Improvement Society at 8 p.m.

THURSDAY—

Women's Hour at 3 p.m.
Prayer Meeting at 8 p.m.
Choir Practice at 8 p.m.

FRIDAY—

Choir Sewing Class at 7 p.m. at St. Michael's,
    Ashwood Road.

SPECIAL ANNOUNCEMENTS

Nov. 3rd Adult Rechabite Tent, 8 o'clock.

Mutual Improvement Society.

Nov. 5th Concert—Knaphill Orchestra
      12th *Ladies' Evening
      19th *Mens' Evening
      26th Lecture— "John Bunyan." Major
            E. Atkins

Dec. 3rd Choir Evening (Musical)
      10th *Ladies' Evening
      31st Coffee Supper and Watchnight
            Service, at 10 p.m.
            * Surprise Evening.

Nov. 25th Monthly Church Meeting at 7.30
            p.m.

CHURCH NOTES.

The outstanding and absorbing event of the past month has been the Mission which was held from October 19th to 26th. Those who were present at the Church Meeting on September 30th, when such definite Divine guidance was realised, would not be surprised at the wonderful week of inspiration which God has given us.

The unforeseen coincidence of a Mission on the very eve of an Election did not appear to diminish in any way the success of the services. The attendance grew steadily each evening reaching its highest point on Thursday. Though Friday's gathering was not as large, for a FRIDAY evening it was a truly remarkable congregation.

As expected, the Rev. Horace Warde, M.A., of Surbiton was with us on the Sunday and Monday ; Dr. Garfield Carse of Finchampstead on Tuesday, Wednesday and Friday ; the Rev. R. B. Jolly, M.A., Vicar of Christ Church, Woking, on Thursday. Unity of purpose made these different ministries as one ; and quiet, sometimes intense spiritual power was maintained throughout. The special significance of Thursday's meeting was as cordially welcomed by Mr. Jolly as by ourselves, and such a demonstration of Christian unity should have far reaching results of the best kind. It should be noted that Dr. Garfield Carse is also a member of the Church of England, and has just received a license to preach from the Bishop of Oxford.

It was the writer's wish that Dr. Carse should take the service on the second Sunday evening, but this being impossible, the Pastor had to be the missioner for the concluding meetings.

With the exception of Friday evening, Mrs. Ashley Cook was able to fulfil her promise to sing at each meeting. It may be confidently believed that, when the results of this Mission

224

Figure 14. Monthly Church magazine from 1931

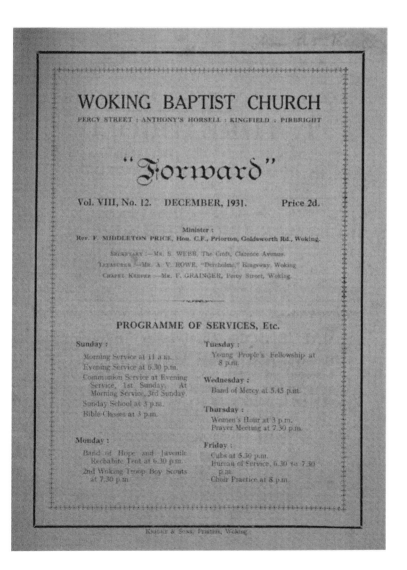

Figure 15. Monthly Church magazine from 1937

WOKING BAPTIST CHURCH

PERCY STREET : KINGFIELD : ANTHONY'S, HORSELL : PIRBRIGHT

"Forward"

| Vol. XIV No. 9 | SEPTEMBER, 1937 | Price 2d. |

PERCY STREET, WOKING

Minister : Rev. S. C. HARRISSON, B.D.,
"Stanmer," Goldsworth Road, Woking.

SECRETARY : MR. W. G. SIMMONS,
"Williston," Ormonde Road, Horsell.

Treasurer : MR. A. V. ROWE,
"Dereholme," Kingsway Avenue, Woking.

PROGRAMME OF SERVICES

Sunday :

Morning Service at 11 a.m.
Evening Service at 6.30 p.m.
Communion Service at Evening Service,
1st Sunday.   At Morning Service,
3rd Sunday.
Sunday School at 3 p.m.
Bible Classes at 3.15 p.m.

Monday :

Band of Hope and Juvenile Rechabite
Tent at 6.30 p.m.
Girls' Auxiliary at 8 p.m.

Tuesday :

2nd Woking Troop Boy Scouts at
7.30 p.m.

Wednesday :

The Fellowship at 7.30 p.m. (Winter
Months).

Thursday :

Women's Meeting at 3 p.m.
Junior Endeavour at 6.30 p.m.
Prayer Meeting at 7.30 p.m.

Friday :

Cubs at 5.30 p.m.
Bureau of Service, by appointment.
Choir Practice at 8 p.m.

Church Meeting last Tuesday of the
Month, at 7.45 p.m.

KINGFIELD

Minister : Rev. F. T. DIMMICK,
4, Vicarage Road, Kingfield.

SECRETARY : MR. W. J. SMITH,
"Westaven," Hoe Bridge Estate, Old Woking.

226

Figure 16. Who's who and weekly services - an extract from August 1965 Newsletter

PASTOR:

Rev. PHILIP L. JONES,
29a Heathside Road, Woking
Telephone—Woking 2053

TREASURER :

Mr. L. GLOSIER,
12 Wheatsheaf Close, Woking
Telephone—Woking 1973

SECRETARY :

Mr. MALCOLM F. SIMPSON
12 Mayhurst Avenue, Woking
Telephone- Woking 60428

DEACONS :

Mr. R. F. BOORMAN
Mr. C. J. DAVIS
Mr. E. C. DOWE
Mr. J. L. GOODE

Mr. C. LANDER
Mr. J. K. LUND
Mr. F. D. PAYNE
Mr. G. PERKINS
Mr. J. B. POTTER

Mr. A. V. ROWE
Mr. W. G. SIMMONS
Mr. A. D. SUSSEX
Mr. T. R. WARREN

MISSIONARIES :

Miss CYNTHIA GOODALL (C.I.M.)
Chefoo School, Tanah Rata
Cameron Highlands, Malaya

Mr. P. and Mrs. S. MURRAY (W.E.C.)
Casilla 41, Melo
Cerro Largo, Uruguay

SERVICES

SUNDAY
Public Worship ... 11 a.m. and 6.30 p.m.
All ages Sunday School ... 9.45 a.m.

TUESDAY
Missionary Working Party *(twice monthly)* 3.00 p.m.
Prayer Meeting and Bible Study 7.45 p.m.

WEDNESDAY
Life Boys 6.15 p.m.
Boys' Brigade 7.30 p.m.
Women's Evening Group *(twice monthly)* 7.45 p.m.

THURSDAY
Women's Fellowship 3.00 p.m.
Girls' Life Brigade 6.00 p.m.

FRIDAY
Boys' Club 7.00 p.m.
"Wondrous Story" Recording Session 7.30 p.m.

SATURDAY
Young People's Fellowship 7.00 p.m.

The Lord's Supper is observed on the first Sunday evening
and the third Sunday morning of each month.

NEWSLETTER EDITOR :

Mr. C. J. DAVIS,
"Elован," Five Oaks Close, St. Johns, Woking
Telephone Brookwood 2217

Annual Subscription 6/- or 6d. per copy

Figure 17. Monthly news letter from 1971, Weekly Announcer from 1975, and Coign Messengers from 1977, 1986 and 1988

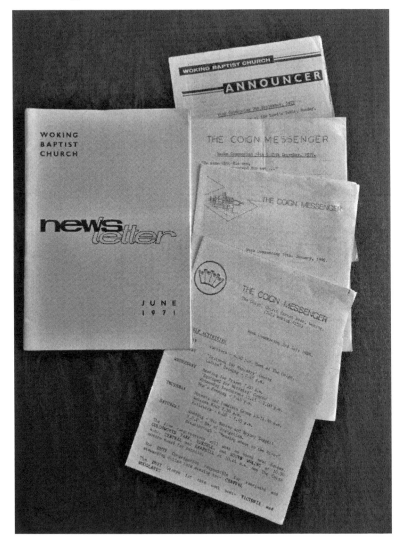

Figure 18, Wondrous Story Choir in Percy St Baptist Church building (mid-60s)

Figure 19, The Coign, exterior (2015)

Figure 20, interior view of The Coign chapel area

WELCOME CHURCH STORY

John Gloster's companion volume, *Welcome, Coign and Woking Baptist Church Story* covers some of the same history as *Church on the Move* but majors on the later years since the Church moved to The Coign, now The Welcome Centre, and continues the story up 2018. John gives a much fuller account of how God has led His people through times of trial, miraculous provisions and light-hearted fun, calling upon the recollections of individuals who have belonged to the Church since those times.

Together, these two volumes provide a fascinating and inspiring account of 140 years of our Church's history – from just eight members in 1879 to over 600 men, women and children at Welcome Church and hundreds more in six Church plants all over the country and in the USA, by 2018.

Copies of *Welcome Church Story* are available through the Welcome Church office and direct from John Gloster, or on Amazon.

Printed by Amazon Italia Logistica S.r.l.
Torrazza Piemonte (TO), Italy

16495218R00144